"Within this book are heartfelt stories
communications from the soul, and
solutions to every day challenges. It is
same pages with these remarkable Soul Coaches.

—DENISE LINN, Founder of Soul Coaching®
www.deniselinn.com

"What lies within this book is a collection of personal, heartfelt stories of triumph, wisdom and joy. Each chapter will lift your spirits! This book has kept me turning the page and not wanting to put it down! I've read the more intimate details of these authors' lives and feel as though I have shared every step of their journey. Not only do they tell their stories but they invite you to take steps to make your life even greater! Simply reading these shared experiences will leave you feeling inspired and uplifted, with changes taking place within you already."

—TERRY BOWEN, Soul Coach, Intuitive Medium, Teacher
www.terrybowen.co.uk

"A wonderfully inspiring collection of heartfelt honesty! I love that this book is about real people, just like you or me, who had an epiphany that came to them from their deeper self. We all desire to live such a life of authenticity and to learn to listen to our inner guidance. The pages of *Soul Whispers III* are scattered with gems of beauty the authors have gained through their soul coaching experiences. As I saw reflections of myself woven within the warmth and wisdom of the authors' words, a sense of comfort filled my heart. I came away from this book feeling fresh, clear and inspired to follow the quiet voice of my soul."

—LIZ WINTER, Writer, Medium, Dream Coach,
Angel Therapist™, Spiritual Teacher
www.lizwintermedium.com

SOUL WHISPERS III

Soul Wisdom for Living
the Life of Your Dreams

Edited by Sophia Fairchild

FOREWORD BY DENISE LINN
Author of *Soul Coaching,*
28 Days to Discover Your Authentic Self

SOUL WINGS® PRESS
Sydney, Australia
Laguna Beach, CA, USA

First Published in the United States by
Soul Wings® Press
Publishing for the Soul®
www.SoulWingsPress.com

The authors of this book do not dispense medical advice nor prescribe the use of any technique as a form of treatment for physical or medical problems without the advice or a physician, either directly or indirectly. The intent of the editor and authors is to offer information of a general nature to help you in your quest for emotional and spiritual well-being. In the event you use any of the information in this book for yourself, which is your personal right, the authors, editor and the publisher assume no responsibility for your actions. All names have been changed to protect client confidentiality, unless otherwise noted.

Excerpts from *Gateway Oracle Cards Guidebook* Copyright © 2012 by Denise Linn, reprinted with permission from the author. Complete card deck available everywhere books are sold, or at www.deniselinn.com.

The terms Soul Coaching® and Interior Alignment® are Federally Registered Trademarks and remain the property of Denise Linn Seminars, Inc. Wherever these terms appear throughout this book the appropriate trademark symbols are implied.

Editorial Supervision by Sophia Fairchild
Book Design by Fiona Raven

Library of Congress Cataloging-in-Publication data
Soul Whispers III : soul wisdom for living the life of your dreams / edited by Sophia Fairchild ; foreword by Denise Linn.
p. cm.
ISBN 9780985186500 (pbk.)
ISBN 9780985186517 (e-book)

1. Self-actualization (Psychology). 2. Self-actualization (Psychology) – Problems, exercises, etc. 3. Spiritual life – Anecdotes. 4. Spiritual life – Problems, exercises, etc. 5. Personal coaching. 6. Success. 7. Change. I. Soul whispers three : soul wisdom for living the life of your dreams. II. Fairchild, Sophia. III. Linn, Denise. III. Title.

BF637.P36 F35 2012   158.1 21 —DC23   2010912072

US EDITION ISBN-13: 978-0-9851865-0-0   ISBN-10: 0-9851865-0-X
UK EDITION ISBN-13: 978-0-9845930-9-5   ISBN-10: 0-9845930-9-8
DIGITAL ISBN: 978-0-9851865-1-7

First Printing December 2012
Printed in the United States of America

This book is dedicated
with love and gratitude to
Denise Linn,
and to all who listen
for the whispers of the soul.

Contents

Foreword

*W*hack! I was hit so hard on my shoulder with the long, hard wooden paddle that the pain radiated into my neck and back. I could hardly breathe as I waited for the sensation to subside.

"God, that hurt! Why did he hit me so hard? Does he dislike me that much?" I thought to myself.

Then a more reasonable part of myself jumped in. I reminded myself that I had moved into a Zen Buddhist monastery to find enlightenment and part of the practice involved Zen discipline. In this particular type of Buddhism, the Zen master hits the Zen students with a stick (called a kyosaku stick) while the students are meditating… as a way of encouraging a focused awareness. The sound of the stick swiftly coming down on a student's shoulder can seem deafening as it echoes off the silent zendo walls and the pain is often searing. The idea is that it spurs the student on to reach enlightenment (or at least not fall asleep while in meditation for up to 16 hours a day).

I reminded myself that getting hit had nothing to do with being liked or not. It was used as a compassionate method of encouraging a flagging Zen practitioner to go deeper. (And actually it was a much better method that the older Zen ways of chopping off a finger or hand to encourage enlightenment.)

Although I lived in the Zen Buddhist monastery for over two years, I never reached enlightenment, but I was able to reach a kind of quietude of the soul. It was also one of the best times in my life. I loved the profound stillness that filled me as I watched a shadow of leaf slowly travel across the wall. It seemed as if time stood still in those moments. (I also learned how to pad my shoulders so that when the kyosaku stick struck the bones of my shoulder, the blow was muffled. This was a secret passed down through the centuries from the older students.)

I had moved into the monastery as an indirect result of a dramatic near-death experience when I was 17 years old. I had been seriously injured after being hit by a car while on my motorbike (as well as further injuries) and had found myself in an emergency ward. While the doctors were frantically trying to revive me (they thought I had gone into cardiac arrest) I found myself whisked out of my body and into a radiantly beautiful dimension of golden light. I knew that I was home… and it was all so familiar. I knew that I had been there before. I never wanted to leave, but I found myself being pulled back into my very damaged body with only a memory of what I'd experienced. I desperately wanted to go back. I intuitively knew that there was a way to get there; I simply had to find it.

From that point forward I was on an odyssey to make my way back to that heavenly place, but without having to die first. The Zen monastery was the first part of this journey. (I had heard that when one reached enlightenment they entered into a land of golden light, so I thought if I reached satori that I could get back there.) After not finding enlightenment in the Zen monastery, my quest eventually led me to train with elders in native cultures around the world. I intuitively felt these people with ancient traditions could provide answers for my long-sought questions. At every juncture in my journey I asked the questions "Who am I? What is truly important in life?"

Eventually the answers began to emerge. For example, I learned that the soul loves the truth and that it's really important to live authentically in accordance with the dictates of your soul and not try to always please others, to the detriment of yourself. I began to share everything that I was learning through seminars I taught and books I wrote. Eventually I distilled what I had learned on my journey into the Soul Coaching® program, which is a certification program that trains people to work with clients one-on-one and also work with groups of people. It was a training that came out of a dream that was born during my years in the monastery.

When I was meditating for long periods of time in the Zen monastery there were times when – instead of focusing on my breath – I dreamed about my future. I'm a bit embarrassed to admit this because we were never supposed to visualize anything. In fact, we were supposed to sit with our eyes half-open to prevent visualizing. (Alas, maybe that's why I got hit so many times.) However, I found that visualization helped me move beyond the pain in my knees from sitting in the lotus position for so many hours. I dreamed about traveling to exotic countries around the world.

I also imagined being a part of a remarkable community of people that wanted to make a difference in the world. And in so many ways, these dreams came true. I did travel the world eventually. And also I did find a loving, gracious community of people who were dedicated to making a difference. The Soul Coaches in this book are a part of that community and it is an honor and delight to have them in my life.

When I'm asked about how I choose who attends my Soul Coaching® program, I answer that it's easy because God only sends me the very best people. You'll find in this collaboration that each of these women stands remarkable in her own right. Indeed the Creator has sent me the best people in the women who are represented in this book. I love these women deeply and profoundly.

Their stories of triumph over adversity and their gracious communications from the soul are moving and heartfelt. Within this book is ancient wisdom as well as modern day solutions to every day challenges. It is an honor and a privilege to share the same pages with these remarkable Soul Coaches. I didn't find enlightenment in the walls of the monastery, but I did seed a dream that blossomed years later... and I'm so thankful.

DENISE LINN
Founder of Soul Coaching®

Launching Your Journey

AFFIRMATION: I am an intrepid traveler, sailing forth into the Universe.

Inner and outer travel are ahead. Get ready, for you are about to embark on a journey. This could be an inner sojourn, a voyage to distant lands, or even a project or idea that is coming to life.

Introduction

The first time I grasped the truth that *I have the power to create the life of my dreams* was the day I pulled out my childhood journals and had the lightning-bolt realization that I was living out, in real life, a fantasy story I had written as a child.

Like all children, I often fantasized about what my life would be like when I grew up. These imaginative stories helped me to get through the tough times when I found myself living in orphanages and children's homes from a very young age.

As a child from the remote bush country of Australia, far from any cities and even more removed from the rest of the world, I visualized myself doing all the most exciting things a small child could imagine – sailing the seven seas, climbing snow-capped mountains, exploring the jungles of Africa, encountering wild animals, crossing the Sahara Desert, seeing the Seven Wonders of the World, studying with holy men and women in India, Peru, Egypt, and other exotic locations, having movie stars for neighbors in America, becoming a writer – and so much more. I wrote most of these childish dreams down in my secret journals as adventure stories.

It wasn't until I was a young adult, many years later, when I pulled out my faded collection of childhood diaries, that I realized I had in fact lived out all of my childhood fantasies, including meeting royalty, something I'd completely forgotten about. This also meant it was time to create some new dreams.

Although I was already a published author by this time, I was suddenly gripped with an irrational fear. Though most writers already live with the trepidation that their writing might be perceived as mediocre and boring, I now developed the additional fear that through the act of writing down my wishful dreams and fantasies; somehow they were all destined to come true! What truly terrified me was the thought that if my writing was bland and uninteresting, that somehow *my life would also turn out that way*. Talk about writer's block!

Yet when I thought about the kinds of passionate, secret dreams I'd had as a child, and how excited I was when I wrote about them, I understood that the magic I'd created in making these dreams spring to life was not in the details of what I wrote, but in the intensity of my feelings in putting them down on paper. It was not only my passionate longing that made my dreams come true, but my willingness to follow my soul's calling, no matter how far out of my comfort zone it took me.

This realization probably didn't make me a better writer, but it did shift the focus of my life's journey to a deeper exploration of life's mysteries. And this led me to study with teachers like Denise Linn, and to the work of helping other writers make their dreams come true. Thus, the book you are holding in your hands is the manifestation of a particularly magical collective dream, a dream visualized by all of its authors.

It has been foretold that the global shift in consciousness, taking place in the year 2012 and beyond, will transform all of our lives. Yet it is also said that because we create our own reality, our outer world is actually a mirror of our inner world. Does this mean that when we see massive changes taking place in both our immediate environment and in the wider world that we are simply perceiving such changes due to our own inner process of transformation? Are these changes in fact the result of all of our collective dreams? And if so, what can we do to ensure that they result in the life we've longed for, both collectively and as individuals – the life of our dreams?

One thing is certain. Change is inevitable. Just as a tiny seed is transformed into a majestic tree through contact with nutrients in the soil and the elements of water and sunlight, so too do we experience growth and transformation through daily contact with the elements, and the people and events which shape our world. In this grand adventure called Life, every incident and relationship we encounter is an opportunity for growth. We can either choose to grow with ease through love and joy, or we can resist change through the experience of fear and struggle.

Denise Linn has always said that we do not need to suffer in order to grow. Thus, we can accept this process of personal transformation and change just as the caterpillar effortlessly transforms into a glorious winged butterfly. And as we learn to love ourselves and accept both our weaknesses as well as our strengths, we expand our capacity to extend this same understanding and compassion towards others. Life becomes sweeter, and we are more capable of accepting inevitable changes with humor and grace.

The truth is that if we are *not* living the life of our dreams, we need to take action to create necessary changes. This may feel uncomfortable at first because it requires pushing ourselves out of our comfort zone, even though for many, this comfort zone may be imbued with the dissatisfaction and pain of unfulfilled dreams. Yet it is only after we have taken this first self-initiated step in the direction of change – towards creating the life of our dreams – that the magic can truly begin. The good news is that we are never alone on this journey.

Constant whisperings from your soul are steadily guiding you towards the life of your dreams. It is our soul which forms the link between our body and spirit, and to the greater forces of the universe. In no small way we are all connected with everything and everyone in the great web of life, which conspires and collaborates with us to support all of our adventures in self-discovery. Thus, ordinary events in our lives can be filled with messages and meaning, if we would only stop to listen. Soul Coaching® provides a comprehensive system of deciphering these truthful and loving messages from our soul.

This book contains a collection of stories and voices gathered from professional Soul Coaches across the globe, with the specific intention of helping you to discover the life of your dreams, one which will bring you the deepest meaning and greatest joy.

As Denise explains, Soul Coaching® is a remarkable program designed for anyone seeking phenomenal spiritual cleansing, renewal and transformation. Its aim is to align one's inner spiritual life with their outer life. It helps to clear away mental, emotional and physical clutter, so that you or your client can hear the secret messages whispered from the soul. It also allows you to discover your true purpose, so you can design a life that supports that purpose.

Soul Coaching® goes beyond the boundaries of ordinary life coaching which focuses on the attainment of goals. It is also not a program of emotional therapy. Soul Coaching® is a guided inward journey to touch the sacred space within. Every Soul Coach knows that their clients are naturally intuitive and resourceful, and understands that each client already has all the answers he or she needs. It is the job of the Soul Coach to create a safe, nurturing space for their clients to discover their own knowledge, while they listen with their heart as well as their ears.

Soul Coaches work in several ways. They may take their clients on inner meditative journeys called Soul Journeys to receive profound answers to heartfelt questions. They can also gently guide their clients through a 28 day program that is a deep inner and outer clutter clearing of the mental, emotional, physical and spiritual aspects of Self, a journey represented by the Medicine Wheel and the ancient elements of Air, Water, Fire and Earth. This 28 day program is often followed by quiet time spent alone on a personal Quest.

By journeying through the pages of this book, you are invited to embark on an exhilarating voyage of self-discovery, learning to decipher your soul's loving messages, helping you unlock the secrets to living the wondrous life you were always destined to live.

Each Soul Coach represented in *Soul Whispers III* brings a unique approach to their Soul Coaching® practice, based on the wisdom and expertise accumulated from a variety of healing modalities and from many different professional fields.

May you be uplifted by their poignant personal stories, and inspired by the wealth of practical exercises and soulful secrets they've shared. Enjoy exploring life-changing techniques, each designed to help you and your clients move through fear to clear your clutter from the inside out, allowing your authentic Self to be fully expressed – and with this new-found clarity, to joyfully participate in the everyday magic of living the life of your dreams.

Let the adventure begin!

SOPHIA FAIRCHILD
Sydney, Australia

MARIANNE MACKENZIE

Austin, Texas, USA

MARIANNE IS AN internationally-certified Soul Coach who specializes in guiding people to create the life of their dreams. Her practice is based on compassion and non-judgment, drawing on a breadth of knowledge gained throughout her multi-dimensional life as a former corporate executive, mother, spiritual seeker, and world traveler. She works with clients to step into the life they deserve, full of abundance, joy, wealth, health, passion and purpose.

In her personal life, she is an author, dancer, dreamer, spiritual partner, video blogger, optimist, introvert, intuitive, voracious reader and recovering perfectionist. She delights in helping clients discover their most authentic self as they come into alignment with their true nature to embrace all the gifts awaiting them. Her goal is to empower and equip people with the tools to identify who they are, who they are not, and who they are meant to be. She offers personal coaching for individuals and groups, live and virtual seminars, and retreats and workshops for those who desire to expand their consciousness and embrace their deepest essence.

To learn more about Marianne, check out her weekly video blog at http://www.MarianneMacKenzie.com and connect with her on www.facebook.com/mariannesoulcoach

Create Your Big Sweet Life!

MARIANNE MACKENZIE

I realized that my breaking point was really my starting point.
The journey was about to begin – a journey to meaning, love and truth.

Perhaps everybody has two lives – the one you have, and the one you desire. At this very moment, you are living the life you've created from within – for better or for worse. Each decision you've ever made has led you right here to this moment. And whether or not this moment is one you consciously choose and enjoy, you did create it with thoughts, beliefs and choices. The beauty of this perspective is that starting now, you can begin to create something new and different if you don't like the circumstances of your current reality.

I didn't always have this awareness. I grew up in a small town where most of the population walked, talked, and worshipped alike. This put me on a direct path to a safe, culture-approved, but small life. There were well-defined boundaries of what was right, wrong and acceptable, and I was expected to stay within them. My role was to simply follow the path my parents and community had taken, without question. Doing something different meant resistance from my community. And because I learned at a very young age how good it felt to please others, I sought their approval often, which meant drowning out the voice of my own wise soul.

Unconsciously, I created a life that fit nicely into this kind of cookie-cutter container, with all the edges tucked inside so nobody could see how flawed I felt. I walked the walk, talked the talk, and was redirected by my peers if I strayed off the path. There were fleeting moments of rebellion and non-conformity, each of them quickly extinguished. But every soul desires freedom to create the life it is intended to live, based on personal truth. And deep inside, I was intent on finding that truth, in whatever form it came.

By my mid-30s, after years of dedication and commitment, I was climbing to the top of the corporate ladder along with my husband, who had an equally demanding career. We were also balancing family life with two chronically overscheduled children. On the surface, we seemed to be living the American dream of achievement, comfort and luxury. Unaware of my personal truths, however, I'd created a life that was out of alignment with my inner wisdom. I was an overachieving workaholic, driven to seek perfection at every turn, no matter the cost to me and my family. I took on far too much, feeling like I had to 'do it all' – all by myself. It seemed like an overwhelmingly heavy load to bear, but I didn't know there was an alternative. I thought it was simply the part I had to play.

This approach kept me disconnected from what my body and heart were trying to tell me, until one day I found myself in the doctor's office on the receiving end of some very bad news. After struggling for more than a year with nagging back pain, I was suddenly facing a grim diagnosis – degenerative disk disease. It was a permanent, irreversible condition in which the disks in my spine would all eventually degenerate and die, one by one. Two of my vertebra, in fact, had already succumbed, and the condition was worsening. What's more, he told me, within a year I would be in a wheelchair unless I underwent surgery to implant a rod in my spine. To me this was not a viable option. I began to look for answers, searching for a way to heal my body and my life. I knew I had to make some serious changes if I wanted to keep my health. My real life and my soul were calling to me, a siren song I could no longer ignore.

I arrived at the conclusion that I could no longer continue on with the life I had created. I had hit a wall, overcome with the knowledge that I had to remake my life in a completely new way. By ignoring the gentle whispers of my heart, life had raised its voice at me so I might listen more closely. I had stopped dreaming, and was merely surviving from one day to the next.

Waking up to the life I had created was painful, and at first I didn't want to take responsibility for it. I sank into a depression, blaming others for my despair and wallowing in self-pity. Over time, the weight of my sadness became so heavy that it broke me. But a transformation was taking place. I began to emerge from the darkness as I realized that my breaking point was really my starting point. The journey was about to begin – a journey to meaning, love and truth.

I had been searching for a new way of living – something that resonated with me on a heart level. Like a guiding light through my clouds of confusion, I discovered teacher and mother of Soul Coaching, Denise Linn. Her message touched the deepest part of me, raising my awareness and helping me connect with my divine personal power. Through the wisdom of many teachers and my own desire to discover my own truth, I peeled back the layers of childhood beliefs and began to understand that I do have the power within me to create the life of my dreams. I like to call this the Big Sweet Life – the most vibrant life you can imagine.

Whether or not you believe right now that your dreams are achievable, know this: If they are your dreams, it is possible to make them come true. I want to guide you to your Big Sweet Life – the best possible one you can imagine. Soul Coaching has been pivotal in waking me up to the beauty and possibility of my own life, helping me to discover my truest desires, and experience them.

Each day presents us with the opportunity to re-create, moving us closer to our dream life. The key is knowing what you want! Perhaps you have been living on autopilot, feeling as though you are just getting by. "What if I don't know what

I want?" you may ask yourself. This is perfectly okay, and even common for many people whose dreams have become obscured by the mundane aspects of day-to-day living. To live, and love, the life of your dreams, you must first become aware of your desires. Then, you can create a plan with clear action steps to take you where you want to go.

Before you begin, it's helpful to first accept where you are in this moment. It is here to teach you. To do this, simply notice your feelings right now, without resistance or judgment. Emotions are one of your greatest allies, and they will point you in the direction of your best life every time. They are the strongest indicator of whether or not you are on the right track.

When we allow ourselves to dream big, our imagination can run wild! This opens up a wellspring of new, divinely-inspired information. It may come through our mind's eye or feelings, and perhaps other senses, including smell and sound. Our intuition engages, and we sense that there is no limit to what our life can be. This happens when we are open to Who We Really Are and what is really possible. This is the space from which we can visualize and create a Big Sweet Life.

Many of us have forgotten our dreams, distracted by the life our culture or family of origin wanted us to live. Often, this is not in alignment with our heart's desire. If we listen to the voice of wisdom in our heart, it will guide us to our own personal truth. Alternatively, we can ignore it and live comfortable, predictable lives. We may do this in an attempt to avoid discomfort, disappointment and perhaps even failure. But in so doing, we also miss the chance to make our wildest dreams come true. What I have discovered from working with hundreds of people is that all of us want them to come true. Whether we believe they can or not, well, that's a different story.

Do you remember your dreams as a child? Can you recall what you wanted to do and be when you grew up? I do, and those dreams were BIG – full of sweetness, excitement and unlimited possibilities. I also remember when they started to diminish, as I stopped believing they could come true. I realize now that I had bought into what my culture was selling – a limited possibility of what my life could be.

It happens to us all. The belief that we can make our dreams a reality fades as we move into adulthood. No matter where you are from, your culture or your religious beliefs, society and your family directly impact your ability to dream big. Some adults have lost the desire or ability to dream altogether. Our dreams are sacred, and when we give up dreaming, we stop believing in and trusting ourselves. This leads us away from the life we intended to live. In order for you to find it, you must first understand Who You Really Are.

Who You Really Are

Who are you? You, my friend, are a Divine immortal Being – a child of the Universe. Your potential is unlimited, and you CAN create everything you imagine. You are perfect for the life you chose to experience! You are not your body, your personality, your past or your future. These are only external, temporary conditions – not a reflection of your timeless nature. You are a spirit of infinite intelligence created of God, or whatever you call your higher power. Within your physical existence, this is referred to as your Soul. It is your essence, your wisdom, and your direct connection to Source.

Experience It!

Now is a great time to sneak a peek at yourself in the mirror. Look directly into your own eyes as you gaze into the mirror and really see your light. Repeat the phrase, "I am a Divine immortal Being." You may need to say it a few times until you feel the shift, as every cell in your body begins to transform with the truth of these words. Denise Linn, my wise friend, mentor and the mother of Soul Coaching says it best: "The Soul loves the truth."

At first, this exercise may challenge you. This is simply the ego, attempting to block you from hearing your inner voice. Be patient. As you learn to connect, that voice will begin to drown out the voice of the ego. We cannot eradicate it, but we can turn down the volume. Unless we do so, we will not live our Big Sweet Life.

Hello ego!

Your ego is only a part of this temporary vehicle, the body. This amazing vehicle allows you to learn and grow while here on Earth. The ego believes that it is in charge, and often we allow it to be. It will do everything in its power to distract and keep you from getting to know your Soul.

The ego can be fearful, jealous, scattered, annoyed, hateful, manipulative, impatient, funny, conceited, full of bravado and downright confusing. You know when you are under the spell of the ego because life is challenging, stressful, painful and defeating. When you listen to your ego, it will consume you with fear, negativity and insecurity. As long as you are alive, your ego is as well. Understanding that the ego is an unavoidable part of our human experience is key. Don't waste your time trying to eliminate your ego. Instead, accept and love this part of you – it is a catalyst for growth.

A teacher once told me that the ego is like a 5-year-old child. Imagine allowing a spoiled, demanding, immature and self-centered child to make your decisions! Allowing the ego to direct your life is like letting the 5-year-old drive your car while the wise You is riding helplessly in the back seat. This helps us realize that we want to be in the driver's seat. When we are stuck in fear, insecurities and doubt, it is because our ego is at the wheel. When this happens, simply let your ego know that you will be driving, and it is welcome to climb into the back seat.

When I find myself under the spell of ego, I take a deep breath and treat myself gently – knowing that berating myself will only strengthen the ego's power. Laughter is the best medicine to counteract this. Here are some ways you might respond when you feel trapped:

- **Laugh at the moment**
  Imagine yourself looking down from above, as a sacred observer witnessing the situation. From this vantage point, you can disconnect from the emotion of the ego and see the humor in the drama.

- **Move your body**
  Movement loosens up the energy surrounding the situation and allows clean, vibrant oxygen and energy to fill your cells. Turn on some music for a dance break!

- **Journal**
  Just picking up the pen and writing your thoughts allows for movement inside your mind. This is a great way to break the spell of the ego. Use colored pencils and pictures to add more power to this option.

- **Reach for a better thought**
  Think of something that makes you feel good – this will help shift your vibration and your state of Being. This is an intermediate level tool that requires 'bliss-cipline': the discipline of consciously choosing good-feeling, blissful thoughts.

Be gentle with yourself. Breaking the spell of the ego is a powerful process that may take time. Joy comes from recognizing the ego's spell and how breaking that spell empowers you.

Big You and Small You

In order to live your Big Sweet Life, you must create it from the Big You – connected to Source, fully plugged in and turned on! Imagine a beautiful Tiffany lamp, with its intricate craftsmanship, adorned with flowers, peacock feathers, dragonflies and butterflies. Even though it isn't turned on, you know there are many colors just waiting to burst forth. As you go to turn on the lamp, you realize that it is not plugged into the wall. Without this connection, the lamp won't shine. The lamp itself is beautiful, yet not nearly as beautiful or as useful as it was intended to be.

This is true for you as well. You must connect to your energy source (your higher power) to fully express what you were designed to do – shine and light up the world. When you turn on your light, you can share a unique creative expression that would otherwise never exist. You are one-of-a-kind, created for a life only you could live.

When you are plugged in, you can fully express your brilliance and live as the Big You. Unplugged, uninspired, and without authentic creative expression, you live as the Small You.

Journal:

Write about a time when you were aware of being or creating from the Big You. What were you doing when you felt this sacred power? How did you feel (emotionally, physically)? Allow yourself to stay in the memory and feeling for as long as you can.

If you are unable to remember a time specifically, that's okay. Instead, imagine yourself as this Big You. What would you feel in your life that you don't feel today? (i.e. focus, confidence, patience, inspiration, energy.)

You created it!

Take a look around your life to get a good sense of what you have created for yourself. As overwhelming as this may seem, it's important to realize you have created it. Your life is a direct reflection of how you are currently using your Divine creativity. As you look at your health, wealth, relationships and career, take notice of what you may have created from the Small You, and what you have created from the Big You. Be gentle with yourself – this is just an opportunity to assess.

Big You creations feel light, yet plunge deep into your heart with a warm, expanded feeling. They give freedom and space to your life. These creations give you energy and resilience. They might include relationships that support, work that invigorates your senses, vibrant health, a connection with nature and gratitude and abundance.

Small You creations often contain a heavy feeling, that of obligation and constant watching or care. Think of home repairs, demanding relationships filled with drama, work projects that exhaust you, your relationship with money (is there ever enough?) and chronically poor health. Most of our life gets filled up with the Small You to-do list.

> ### Following Your Bliss
>
> AFFIRMATION: *My soul sings with joy.*
>
> *Do what gives you joy. Celebrate and have fun. You do not need to suffer to grow — in fact, true happiness comes from following the dictates of your soul. Take steps today to expand your joy. You don't need to do it all at once, but you do need to start.*

If being the co-creator of your life is a new concept, just sit with the idea for a minute. This awareness is a paradigm shift that transfers the power to create your Big Sweet Life from the outside world and external influences directly into your hands.

Journal:

Explore your life and ask yourself the following questions to better understand why you might have created specific things or moments in your life. Do this quickly as your first instincts will be most authentic. Here are a few examples:

Example 1: An Argument
- Why might I have created this argument?
  Creating this argument took the focus off the fact that I didn't plan enough time to get all the things done today that I desired.

- How did creating this argument serve/work for me?
  It allowed me to speak my frustration out loud and get it off my chest.

- How did this argument make me feel?
  Forceful during the argument and then embarrassed to handle my frustration at myself by giving it to someone else.

- Did I create this from the Small me or Big me?
  I created this argument from the Small me.

Example 2: Stressful Situation
- Why might I have created this stressful situation?
  Creating this stressful situation is what I do when I need extra adrenaline to get the task done. I work best when there is stress and pressure.

- How did creating this stressful situation serve/work for me?
  I realize now that I'm using unhealthy energy to get me through my tasks. It isn't healthy and I am not really my best self when I create this kind of stressful situation.

- How did this stressful situation make me feel?
  I felt tight, agitated and impatient. I can feel my whole body react when I create stressful situations. This is not a healthy creation for me.

- Did I create this from the Small me or Big me?
  I created this stressful situation from the Small me.

Example 3: 'Me Time'
- Why might I have created 'me time?'
  I created "me time" from a deep part of me asking to put me first.

- How did creating 'me time' serve/work for me?
  Creating "me time" is something I did to recharge myself, re-focus my thoughts and quiet my mind.

- How did 'me time' make me feel?
  It makes me feel valued and worthy. When I take 'me time', a deep sense of relaxation and contemplation happens. My body, mind and soul expand and soften. Although it isn't always easy to carve out 'me time', when I do, it feels amazing!

- Did I create this from the Small me or Big me?
  This is a Big me creation.

Now it's your turn. Take a moment and ask yourself the following:
- Why might I have created _____?
- How did creating _____ serve/work for me?
- How did _____ make me feel?
- Did I create this from the Small me or Big me?

Repeat each question until you exhaust your list of issues. Use these quick questions throughout your day to assess and better understand what you are creating and if it is coming from the Small or Big me. Just the very awareness these questions bring to your conscious mind will create a shift in your life. As you become more intentional, you gain authentic power, creating from conscious choice.

The Big You is conscious of the creations brought into your life. Most of us create unconsciously until we experience enough suffering and frustration that we decide there must be another way.

The Bubble

Imagine that a bubble represents your current life, and you live inside the bubble. Everything in your world fits within it: your family, friends, career, home, cars, vacations, income, debts, education, self-image and beliefs. Essentially, this bubble represents everything you have experienced and believe: all of your creations, conscious or unconscious.

Your dreams – things you have not yet experienced – are just outside the Bubble. These are what we reach for when we think of a better life. They may include anything that improves your life in some way: better health, supportive relationships, more money, a bigger house, more time for vacation, self-care, and work that feeds your heart and soul, spirituality, a luxury car, and a fabulous family. These things sometimes feel difficult to have, and we may not know how to bring them into our life. You may have heard this referred to as 'manifesting.' The amazing truth is, you are a manifesting machine – everything in your life is your manifestation. So why is it so hard to have the things we dream about?

The answer is simple. We have constructed walls that often times keep us stuck in the same place. The outer edges of the Bubble of your life-experience keep you from achieving the dreams that lie just beyond your current reach. Expanding the walls allows new experiences to fit inside.

Baggage and Barriers

The walls of your Bubble represent what is holding you back. They are composed of Barriers and Baggage. Baggage is the pain and sorrow from your past – those things you bring forward into the present. Think of them as stones you pick up along the journey of your life. Rather than observing them and then putting them down, you place them in your sack. One or two stones aren't a problem, but most of us carry many into each new day. A sack full of stones makes it difficult to reach for our dreams, exhausting us and slowing us down in our everyday life. Each stone may represent something our parents did or didn't do, a betrayal, a sibling rivalry, a boss's behavior, schoolyard bullying, or harsh words you haven't forgiven.

They can also represent issues around money, sex, or health. If you struggle with chronic pain or illness, you may be carrying the stone of weak health. For instance, I grew up being told that I was highly susceptible to strep throat. Sadly, not knowing any better, I accepted that as truth. Quickly I formed a belief, which showed up again and again because I included it in my Bubble. When I realized I was carrying this stone and decided to take it out of my sack, my health improved. I have had clients and friends do this with ailments such as migraines, colds, bronchitis, cancer, accidents, back pain, ulcers, allergies and asthma. To change your outer experiences, you must first change your inner thoughts and beliefs. The simple act of recognizing the relationship between your beliefs and your experiences will begin to alter your perception of your experiences. After that, changing your beliefs becomes easier and easier.

Journal:

Take a moment to think about the stones you are carrying in your Bubble. Are there any stones that you have decided to throw out of your sack? Which stones do you want to keep? You may not know how to let go of the stones you currently have. That's okay. At this time, the important part is the recognition that they are there.

Barriers are things that are keeping you from moving forward and expanding your Bubble. Barriers, like Baggage, are related to beliefs formed from past experiences. Barriers are a creation of the Small You. When you decide to break through the Barriers to improve and grow your life, there is discomfort. If you are conscious during this process and prepare, you can face the challenge head on and push forward through it. If you are unconscious in your approach, however, the discomfort acts like an invisible force field, pushing you back into your comfort zone.

Don't worry about working out all the details in advance. As you identify the general direction in which you want to go, you can set goals for yourself in alignment with your core desires. Allowing for adjustments as you notice signs along your path is instrumental in loving the end result, which may look different from what you imagined. As you discover what gives you joy, you also develop clarity about your desires, which is the foundation for your Big Sweet Life.

I invite you to join me and together we will discover your personal truth and your dreams, identify what Barriers and Baggage are holding you back and expand your life to include fully living the Life you were born to live. You are worth every ounce of time and energy that this choice requires. Come on my friend – YOUR life is waiting for you!

∽

FELICIA MESSINA-D'HAITI

Waldorf, Maryland, USA

FELICIA MESSINA-D'HAITI is an Energy Empowerment Practitioner, working with clients who are eager to create balance and embrace positive healing energies in their bodies, minds and environments.

As a child, Felicia had an interest in changing her environment, moving furniture, and changing the colors and art work in her room. This continuing passion combined with Felicia's advanced studies in Art, Art History and Education led her through several transformations and revelations about her own journeys of discovery and to her current mission of helping people to clear the physical, mental, emotional and spiritual blockages that hold them back from living a life of freedom, balance, joy and where their soul leads them.

Felicia is a certified Usui Reiki Master/Teacher and Level 1 Hatha Vinyasa Yoga Teacher. She is an Advanced Practitioner of Interior Alignment® and Medicine Wheel Feng Shui, through The International Institute of Interior Alignment® Feng Shui & Space Clearing; a Soul Coach and Past Life Coach through the International Institute of Soul Coaching®, and a Gateway Dreaming™ Coach and Master Oracle Card Practitioner, certified by Denise Linn.

In working with Felicia, clients receive individualized services that combine elements from her training, experience and intuition. Felicia works with an international client base, with individuals and groups, in person and online. She gives presentations and workshops for conferences, schools, businesses, and other organizations.

Felicia resides in Maryland with her husband and four young children. For more information, contact Felicia at www.feliciadhaiti.com

Moving Through Fear

FELICIA MESSINA-D'HAITI

During Fire Week, we examine and confront our fears, take risks,
develop faith, learn how to be present and so much more.

*H*ave you ever sat outside on a warm, sunny day and seen nothing but the darkness of your mind, felt the heaviness of your heart, having absolutely no idea what path you were about to take? Several years ago, I sat at a conference in Florida, staring at a blank piece of paper, not knowing what to write; then writing a few words, erasing them, balling up the paper, thinking to myself, "Will I ever get this letter finished?" My heart kept telling me to write it, get it over with and mail it. But my mind was telling me that if I mailed it I'd be a big disappointment, that I'd be a failure and everyone would know it. How could I have invested so much time and energy into this work to just walk away from it?

Until that time, I couldn't even see the path that led me there. I just knew that I was not happy and needed to make a change, but was afraid to. Though I was unhappy, I was comfortable with my discomfort. I knew what to expect and could predict how events would unfold. I knew what I had to do, how and when to do it. As I look back on that point in my life, I'm reminded of a quote by Anaïs Nin: "And the day came when the risk to remain tight in the bud was more painful than the risk it took to blossom." And as I look back, I feel gratitude for the people who supported and encouraged me to move through my fears to create a new life for myself.

More than six years ago, I was exhausted and overwhelmed. I was working full time as a public school art teacher, had three young children and was a student in a Ph.D. program writing my dissertation. I was involved in numerous activities and organizations, and negotiated everything around my husband's changing work schedules. With all of this going on, I had no time to reflect on or assess what my true direction was. I was traveling on an educational path that I had laid out for myself before having our first child, and before I was working full time as a teacher. Yet, I felt obligated to finish the dissertation, keep all of my other obligations, memberships and activities. Most of all, I wanted to appear happy doing it all. To me, not accomplishing all of the goals I had set for myself meant I was a disappointment, a flop, a letdown. Failure was not something that I valued, so I continued on my path no matter how miserable I was.

Interestingly enough, it never occurred to me that I had the power to change my path. I only knew that I was frustrated, depressed and tired – always tired. I was finding less and less joy in my life. There was less and less time to take care of myself. I was off-balance, so trapped in my daily routines that I didn't even see how unhappy I was. My original intention had been to teach for only a few years, just until I finished my dissertation, but the 'only a few years' turned into nearly a decade. I remained teaching at a school in which I was unhappy because I imagined it too difficult to move to another school. What if I made a change and was even more miserable? At least I knew what disappointments and hardships I would face there. I was already prepared for them. I finally did move to a new school. Then, after making the transition, wondered why I was still so unhappy. I continued moving on this endless treadmill until one day it hit me… *What am I doing? Why am I not happy? What is wrong with me? What can I do about this?*

When I turned to colleagues and friends for advice, they suggested that I was just tired; I just needed some rest. I went to a medical doctor who suggested I may be depressed and who said, "Of course, you are tired. You have a full-time job, three children and you're trying to write a dissertation. What do you expect?" This was true, but there was something else. I hadn't realized it yet, but I felt trapped in my career and educational choices. Perhaps I didn't recognize the feeling of being trapped because I had never felt that way before.

Until then, I had been fearless. I had traveled in other countries alone, changed my college studies from a pre-medical program to art history, and took challenging jobs and classes – all without fear. I was willing to try things at which I wasn't sure I would succeed. In fact, it never occurred to me that I would fail at anything. I simply went where my heart and intuition led me. Friends would often tell me they couldn't believe I did something, or went somewhere alone, because it seemed so scary, but I did not understand what they meant. But now, things were different, and I didn't know why. I did not recognize that it was fear keeping me on this path of general unhappiness.

I thought maybe I was just not organized enough; maybe I needed a new system (although I am one of the most organized people I know.) So, I began to look for a new and better system. While searching, I came across several websites with courses to help women become more organized and lead more joyful lives. One of those was called *Change Your Life Challenge* by Brook Noel. It was a 70-day makeover process for women. I bought and read the *Change Your Life Challenge* book, and followed the program.

One component of the program was a daily affirmation email which uplifted me when I read it each day. Because I had not reached the point where I was examining my own thoughts in a meaningful way, I did not realize then that these emails were changing my outlook on life by changing my thoughts from a negative to a more positive outlook. Every morning, I couldn't wait to open my email just to read the daily affirmation and set my intentions and mood for the day. After working with the program for a while, I saw that the author was sponsoring a weekend conference in Orlando in the fall of 2006. What a wonderful getaway! So, I signed up to go.

During the conference, I met a wonderful group of supportive women, each at different stages in their lives. There were no judgments, no criticism within the group. We had opportunities to attend workshops and share ideas. During one conversation, a woman said to me, "If you are not happy in your dissertation program, change it. Why are you still in a program that does not appear to be fulfilling your life?" I thought really hard about why I was still in this program after nearly 10 years. My biggest and perhaps only reason for staying was that I didn't want to be known as someone who didn't finish what she started. I also felt that I had already invested so much money and other resources into the program that it would be a huge let-down to my family.

I thought of a quote used in one of the affirmation emails: "Just because you bought a ticket doesn't mean you have to stay for the second act" (unknown). When did I decide that I couldn't change my mind mid-stream? I had already done so dozens of times, including in college when I changed my program of studies from pre-medicine to art history. I had seemingly changed course with grace and ease on other occasions, why now was I filled with fear?

So, I moved from a vague feeling that something was making me unhappy, to thoughts that it was my own actions that were making me depressed. It was my stubbornness and limited vision of myself and my life that was keeping me trapped on a path that was no longer the right one for me. With all my feelings of depression, the anger at myself for taking so long to complete the program and increasing feelings of apathy about my program, I imagined I should have been thrilled to make this discovery. Yet, I was terrified. What was I afraid of? – disappointing my family and friends, worried that other people would think I was a quitter, deeply concerned that my advisor who had worked so hard with me would never understand nor forgive me for leaving the program? I had to weigh the depth of my desire to live a life true to myself, versus my projections of what other people would think of me. Looking back, I also believe that part of my fear was giving up something that had taken up so much of my life, that there would be a huge gap that I wouldn't know how to fill. What if I made the decision to start something new and then was still horribly miserable? What then?

After I made the decision to withdraw from the program, I needed to take an action. I felt that if I didn't do something, all of these thoughts would just remain thoughts. What would I do? Would I slip back into what was comfortable but not joyful for me? Did I believe I deserved to be happy? A suggestion was made that I write and mail a 'resignation' letter that weekend. The letter was to be written to my advisor, informing her that I was leaving the Ph.D. program. That would be a definite action that I couldn't take back once I had mailed the letter.

Well, writing that letter was the most difficult document that I had ever written. I sat outside in a comfortable spot for what seemed like forever as I tried to put the words together for this resignation letter. I agonized over each word, thought about its meaning and how it would be interpreted. Finally, I finished it, addressed it and walked around with it for a bit. Then, it was popped in the mail at the hotel on the morning of the last day of the conference. Interestingly enough, I have absolutely no remembrance of what I wrote. This letter that I mailed six years ago was a major turning point in my life.

That same morning that the letter was mailed, I announced my decision to the other women in the group at the conference, telling them that I had written and mailed the letter; and what it meant for me. They applauded and supported my decision to make myself happy. Making an announcement to a room full of strangers was the easy part. But the thought of my advisor reading the letter, or having to tell my dad, my husband, or anyone who knew me back home what I was doing, terrified me. I don't even know if terror is the right word; it could be any of these words: fear, horror, fright, dread, shock, panic, alarm. But was it any worse than the constant but subtle upset stomach, back pain, and the grinding of my teeth while I slept that my husband would often tell me about? Was this fear worse than the headaches, depression, anxiety or any of the silent suffering I had endured over the past few years?

I kept thinking about all of the money I had invested, all of the sacrifices that I and my family had made. What was I doing? Would everyone tell me how stupid I was, how ridiculous it was to give up such an opportunity, that it would effectively kill my current career or any chances of advancement in education? I had never felt such an extreme level of discomfort. In my younger days, I had been fearless. I'd traveled throughout Europe and Egypt, often alone. I was independent, courageous, and strong. I took actions and volunteered for activities without thinking of what might go wrong, or how scary it might be. What had changed? Were there so many unknowns in my life that I couldn't bear to have this one uncertainty, even though I was unhappy in what was certain?

Well, of course, it turned out that every person I told of my decision seemed almost relieved. They just wanted me to be happy. It was my fear of what they would think of me that had held me back – not them. It also turned out that the letter I agonized over that beautiful day in Florida somehow never made it to my advisor, so I had to tell her again anyway. She was also supportive, helped me to 'graduate' with a degree reflective of the work that I had completed, and she still keeps in touch with me to find out how my new path in life is going.

So now I had arrived at a point at which I knew where I *didn't* want to go, but I didn't know where I was going either. I signed up with a life coach to help me find a different career path. She asked me to make a list of all the things I liked to do so I could 'discover' which career path to follow. Well, my list included many things, such as interior design, feng shui, aromatherapy, numerology, photography, Reiki and astrology. In my mind, I was sure that I would never find something that incorporated all of these things. But, at the direction of the coach, I began to do research in hopes of finding this new career that would make me happy.

During my research, I discovered Denise Linn's School of Interior Alignment. The studies included feng shui, photography and color, aromatherapy, astrology, numerology, Reiki and many more things that truly fascinated me. When I saw the website, it somehow seemed familiar to me. I knew I had read about Interior Alignment somewhere else. I began looking through some of my books on feng shui and re-discovered *Feng Shui for the Soul,* by Denise Linn. This was one of my favorite books that I had been reading and using to make changes in my own home! *That was it! Wow!* The Universe delivered. It was in the late summer of 2007 when I found Denise Linn's website and reconnected with her book.

That same week, Interior Alignment practitioners were gathered for a conference. I emailed several of the teachers and spoke with one on the phone. Everything I learned was encouraging. The teachers were open and welcoming. The teacher I spoke with on the phone stated that once I had met the right teacher for me, I would know it. Shortly, thereafter, I connected with one of Denise's Master Educators who would become my teacher for the certification course. I then embarked on an online program of study.

Underlying my studies was a thread of inner development and growth. I needed to constantly push myself out of my own way and out of a place of fear. This fear still caught me off guard, because I thought I had left it in Florida. Still, I heard my inner thoughts asking me if I knew what I was doing; if I was doing it right;

> ### Igniting Courage
>
> AFFIRMATION: *I am strong, valiant, and courageous.*
>
> *Move forward fearlessly. Gather your inner forces and take a risk. Speak up for yourself by honoring your truth. This isn't the time to be timid or hold back. Go forward gallantly with your banner of truth waving in the wind. You are a light bearer for others.*

if I was good enough. How could I switch careers and be successful? What if I switched and wasn't successful? These thoughts were often present; however, I was so excited about my studies that I was able to move past these thoughts. All of the information seemed intuitive, as if I had already learned it. It came easily, and I enjoyed making changes in my own home and for some of my friends as I progressed through the course.

While studying Interior Alignment, I noticed that my teacher was also conducting an online course called a 28 day Soul Coaching program. It looked interesting so I signed up for the class. That month was one of the most amazing and enlightening ones I'd had in quite some time. Not only did it incorporate clutter clearing on the physical level, which I loved, but emotional, intellectual and spiritual clutter clearing as well. I discovered many new things, including taking a good look at how critical and demanding I had been of myself, and how I had settled on but could easily re-write the meaning I gave events and decisions in my life. During 'Fire Week' of the program, I began to examine and pull apart my fears, learning to take risks and regaining my creative and adventurous spirit.

At last, I began to see how all the puzzle pieces fit together, bringing me to this point. I realized that instead of appreciating what my past experiences had given me, I was angry with myself for 'wasting time' and changing my career direction 'too many' times. Now, I was beginning to peel back the layers of how my decisions were all related, and how I could not have arrived at my current spot without previously going to the other places I had been. I was finally beginning to appreciate my journey and the experiences that shaped my present life.

Since then, I have participated in the 28 day Soul Coaching program a number of times. Each time, I discover a new layer of myself. The most difficult and most meaningful part of the program for me was, and continues to be, Fire Week, during which we clear our spiritual self. During this week, we examine and confront our fears, take risks, develop faith, learn how to be present and so much more. Every time I go through the program, I uncover and conquer yet another layer of my fears.

When I think of where I am now in my journey, another quote comes to mind: "Your current safe boundaries were once unknown frontiers" (unknown). I realize how far I have come and yet how far I still want to go. I know that it is OK for me not to know how I am going to get there. My belief that the Universe will provide only what is in my highest good will belay inaction due to any fears I possess. Each time I step beyond my perceived limits, I see how much I have learned. I realize that life is more about the journey and our experiences and growth. I am not the same person I was a few years or months or hours ago. With each new thought, action and experience, I evolve into the person I am meant to be.

I have also realized that the Soul Coaching programs and processes were what I was meant to find and combine with the other energy work I had learned. Working with our mental, emotional, spiritual and physical selves is a complementary extension of clearing the physical space of one's environment. One cannot separate self from environment. Just as we have an impact on our lived spaces, our environment affects us as well. As a Soul Coach, I now assist others in discovering their more authentic self as I continue to encounter mine.

I've often heard people say that fear is False Evidence Appearing Real, but it is more than an appearance; it is the feeling that matters. It is a feeling that can be so deep that it can paralyze you, preventing you from making decisions or changes in your life. A Merriam-Webster definition of fear is that it is "the emotion experienced in the presence or threat of danger," or "an uneasy state of mind usually over the possibility of an anticipated misfortune or trouble." Fear is designed to protect us, but sometimes we need to protect ourselves from our fearful feelings. A life without a certain amount of fear is a life without risk. And taking risks involves trust. It is during Week Three – Fire Week of the Soul Coaching program that we learn to listen to our inner voices, take risks, change our routines and habits, examine our fears, and access spiritual allies.

I now look forward to Fire Week with great anticipation, each time I take one of my clients through the 28 days of Soul Coaching. It is a wonderfully profound experience to guide another soul in peeling back the layers of fear, some realized and some not, in order to create a life that brings joy, freedom and peace. It is during this magical time that we are empowered to take action, to come even closer to living the life of our dreams!

Connecting to Your Spirit

Death is not the biggest fear we have; our biggest fear is taking the risk to be alive – the risk to be alive and express what we really are.

—DON MIGUEL RUIZ

In the 28 day Soul Coaching program, there is a week dedicated to the Spiritual aspect of self. This is symbolized by the element of fire. During this time, use the energy of fire to step into trust and faith, learn to hear and listen to your inner voices, examine and release your fears, change your routines, take risks, and activate your creativity in order to craft the life of your dreams.

One exercise to begin with is to make a list of all of your fears. Here, be as specific as possible. In a journal, write 'I am afraid of _____.' List everything that comes to mind. Do not stop to think about what you are writing; just write until you cannot think of anything else to write.

Next, examine your list; look at each item that you wrote. Decide which one thing from the list you are most afraid of. Write that on a separate page. Then, imagine all possible scenarios related to that fear. What is the worst possible scenario related to that fear? In my case: what was the worst possible thing that could happen to me by leaving my dissertation program? Perhaps that others would be upset with me or that I would limit my chances of advancement in my field? When I think about these things now, I see that I cannot live my life by what I perceive others' wishes for me to be, nor can I live my life worried about what others may think of me or my decisions. In looking at advancement in my career, was I even going to stay in the same field?

Once you imagine the worst possible scenario, list all of the positive or valuable experiences that could result from that scenario. This may be the most difficult part of the exercise, but it is valuable in helping to deconstruct the fear. I knew that I had gained a great deal of knowledge in my graduate program, knowledge that

I had already implemented in the classroom and in my own life. When I closely examined my concentration, I realized that I was examining how we are affected by our environment. Many of the books I read in this area of education have direct relation to feng shui and how we design our environments to best support our goals. I was meant to take a meandering path to a life of healing work, to gather the knowledge and experiences over those years. No time is ever wasted time.

Once we have thought about and deconstructed our fears, another valuable exercise is to take risks and action. Some of us, especially those who are recovering perfectionists, can spend time thinking of a million different action plans and scenarios trying to perfect what has not happened and what is not really in their control. The best way to truly know if you have conquered a fear is to take some type of action. For me, it was writing that letter and telling my conference group that I was changing my path.

Oftentimes, we already know what we need to do in order to make a change in our lives. We know what we want; we can see the end result. Yet the step between where we are now and where we want to be appears to be an impossible one. This is the time when we need to break down that giant leap into baby steps. Write down your desired end result. Then write down smaller actions or midpoints to reach that end. If those steps feel too big, break them down to even smaller steps until they feel manageable. Make a commitment to yourself to take at least one step per day.

Most importantly, celebrate your movement, your action, on each step. Fear works to paralyze us. It works to keep us from taking risks, from thinking 'outside the box'. Taking action diminishes your fears and builds self-confidence. Celebrate each of your successes, and your perceived failures, as you move toward living the life of your dreams.

Bibliography

Linn, Denise. *Feng Shui for the Soul*. Hay House, 1999.
Noel, Brook. *The Change Your Life Challenge*. Champion Press, 2005.

Letting Go

AFFIRMATION: I surrender joyously to the ebbing and flowing of life.

Surrender. Relinquish control and allow Spirit to take over. You don't need to do everything by yourself. All is well. It's time to just let it all go and enjoy the ride! Doing so gives others permission to let go in their own lives.

LOES VAN MIERLO
California, USA

LOES IS WHAT you'd call a woman of the world. Originally from the Netherlands and currently residing in California, she has lived in six countries on three continents. She is always looking for new experiences, knowledge and friends. During her travels she picked up many skills, including Ayurvedic massage and Reiki in India, traditional Thai massage in Thailand, leading a dreamboard circle in the Philippines and how to fix practically anything with Duct tape.

Loes holds two Master degrees, one in Finnish language and culture studies from the University of Groningen (Netherlands) and one in European culture studies from the University of Goettingen (Germany). After various jobs, including teaching and sales, she found herself a career in online marketing. She worked for one of the fastest growing internet companies in Europe before being hired by Google. Following her passion for coaching, Loes took the leap of setting up her own business and hasn't looked back. She loves helping people to get clarity about what's holding them back from living the life they want, and together they transform those insights into actions.

Loes works with people from all over the world. If you would like to learn more about how Loes could support you to invite the future of your dreams, please visit her at her website www.loesvanmierlo.com

Inviting Your Future

LOES VAN MIERLO

*Dreamboards are magical. Something extraordinary happens
when you set the intention that your intuition will guide you
to the images that hold a message for you.*

"Here's to our dreams!" I said out loud while raising my glass as we all toasted to our dreams. I looked around the room at the women who had gathered in my apartment building in Manila, Philippines, one Sunday afternoon. I was amazed by the group that had shown up. We were eight women from eight different countries, some of whom had met before, and some who hadn't. We had just spent a few hours together, quietly leafing through magazines, cutting out images which somehow caught our attention and in some way spoke to us, then pasting them onto a large poster board.

Afterwards we sat around in a circle, while one of the women used her Tibetan singing bowls to guide us on a meditation to connect with the messages on our dreamboards. Everyone who wanted to was invited to share her experience, and in the end we shared a glass of wine to celebrate our dreams. Some of these women will never meet again, but in opening up and letting their dreams come to the surface, and in voicing them out loud, often for the very first time, a special bond was created between all of us. Years later, one of the attendants described that afternoon as "a time when I felt free to dream, free to believe that anything is possible, and safe to be completely myself." Dreaming is both powerful and empowering, and dreaming together even more so.

I had been making dreamboards or soul boards, as I like to call them, for years already, always on my own. There was a time when I would make one every month, on the evening of the full moon. It had become a ritual, a sacred ceremony, to spend some time by myself, leafing through magazines, cutting and pasting, dreaming away. I would light a candle and some incense, pour myself a glass of wine and put on some soft music in the background. I loved those hours, in which nothing else existed but collecting images and arranging them in such a way that I could decipher the messages they held for me. Time stood still as I connected to a part of me that only seemed to emerge while making intuitive collages.

It wasn't until I moved to the other side of the globe and was feeling lonely that

I decided to organize a dreamboard circle as a way to meet new friends. I checked with a few women I had met to see if they would be interested and I was thrilled when they were. Some of them asked if they could bring friends. And so it happened that one Sunday afternoon, my first soul board circle took place. It was an afternoon that would change my life.

I had been feeling very unhappy in my job (the same online marketing job that had brought me to the Philippines in the first place) for quite some time already, and my life there had turned out to be a lot more challenging than I had expected it to be. I realized I needed a change, but had no idea where to look for it. The soul board I made that afternoon clearly showed me what I longed for the most: to enrich my soul, to do work that was close to my heart, passion and clarity; a sumptuous life, colorful and abundant; a feeling of peace, to connect with my inner wisdom; to create and to share. Looking at my board, I couldn't believe I hadn't realized this before. Seeing it before me, in images, there was no doubt in my mind that these were all essential elements of my dream life. The big question was: how could I create that dream life?

A few days later, while journaling, it suddenly all became clear. Becoming a certified Soul Coach with Denise Linn had been on my wish list for a couple of years already, but the combination of the tuition fee and the airfare had always been enough to push that dream to the back of my mind. I realized this was the change I had been looking for, the way I could create the life I had envisioned on my dreamboard! I promised myself that my next bonus at work would go towards making this dream come true. The simple act of committing myself to my dream felt wonderful and exciting and empowering, even though I wasn't eligible for a bonus for at least another four months.

The next day I got an invitation from my manager for a meeting, but oddly enough he didn't mention what it was about. Imagine my surprise when he announced how much my bonus was and that I would see it on my next pay check. Normally I was eligible for a bonus once every six months, but this was my second one in just three months! Of course I didn't mention any of this to my manager, as it was clear to me that this extra, unexpected bonus was a sign that I was heading in the right direction. It is my belief that by fully committing myself to making my dream come true, the universe provided me with the finances to make it happen. Straight away I registered for the first Soul Coaching course of the new year, before I had a chance to allow doubt to creep in and change my mind. The next spring I travelled overseas to Summerhill Ranch, on the central coast of California, to become a certified Soul Coach.

As I mentioned, that Sunday afternoon in Manila was to change my life. The board I made during the dreamboard circle showed me things I had been seeing glimpses of for a long time, something I already knew deep down inside, but had been afraid to admit. It stirred something in me, feelings of hope and faith that I couldn't ignore. I had no idea how I would make it happen; I just knew I would, somehow. I had found my Personal Legend, as Paulo Coelho calls it in his book *The Alchemist*. The idea that I might not be able to pull it off didn't even occur to me. I just focused on figuring out how I could make the life that I envisioned on my soul board become a reality.

> *And, when you want something,*
> *all the universe conspires in helping you to achieve it.*

—PAULO COELHO

Dreamboards are magical. Not in the way a genie in a lamp is magic, or in the sense that you make one and that's it, you can just sit back and wait until you get what you want. But something extraordinary definitely happens when you sit down and set the intention that your intuition will guide you to the images that hold a message for you.

During my certification training at Summerhill Ranch, there was one afternoon scheduled for making a Soul Coaching Collage. Armed with a big poster board, scissors, glue and a stack of magazines and other images, I sat down at my favorite table in the cabana under the grape vines. The sun was warming my skin, I could smell the lavender around me and the birds were happily chirping their songs. It was the first time I had ever created a soul board outdoors, and it felt as though the elements that surrounded me were adding their energy to my board. Having created dreamboards for years, I considered myself somewhat of a dreamboard veteran. But at Summerhill Ranch I learned a new way of looking at my soul boards, which helped me to connect with my board on an even deeper level.

Feeling is elemental was a phrase that appeared on my board, pasted over a two-page image of ancient trees. In fact, a lot of images of different nature scenes turned up on my board. They symbolized my love for nature and how I feel better when I connect with the elements, as well as my love for traveling and living in different countries. *The spirit of adventure is forever young* and *Choose your own adventure* reminded me that in my heart and soul I'm an explorer, always looking for new places, new experiences, new discoveries and new connections. Even now, years later, from time to time I look at the board I made that afternoon, and it continues to give me inspiration and insight.

A few nights after creating our Soul Coaching Collages, I learned a new way to affirm the things that had shown up on my soul board, and fell in love with the process immediately. I got together with a few fellow course participants and we imagined that it was one year ahead into the future. The date was the same, but it was one year later. We sat around the big dining table with a nice glass of organic Californian wine and instead of talking about what all of us wanted to do after we returned home as certified Soul Coaches, we each described in detail all the wonderful things that had happened to us in the year that had passed.

At first I thought it would feel a bit silly to pretend we were a year ahead, describing events that might never happen. But soon everyone really got into it and envisioned the things we were longing for the most. We listened to each other's stories, celebrating the professional glories and personal successes the others had experienced. We got excited about new romantic relationships that had been formed and we ooh'd and aah'd about babies that had been born in the past year. We asked each other details about the goals we had reached and the wonderful things we had accomplished and the magic we had created. We really imagined what it all felt like, and shared in the enthusiasm, passion, love and adventures we wished for ourselves.

I talked about things that had shown up on my dreamboard a few days earlier as if they had already happened and in doing so, I felt as if they had come true already! It was the same for the other ladies at the table. Our eyes were shining, and we were all beaming. We could barely contain our excitement. It felt so real! In pretending to be a year into the future and looking back on the things I had done during the past 12 months, I started to really look forward to the year ahead and all the things I had seen myself create in that time. Instead of feeling overwhelmed or doubtful if I could do this, I couldn't wait to start and make it happen.

Exactly one year later, I pulled out the journal I had kept at Summerhill Ranch and read back what I had envisioned for myself that night. I was amazed to see how much of it had really come about! Some things had occurred literally as I had imagined them. I had envisioned myself in a new home with wooden floors and the sun streaming in through my windows. But it wasn't until I was reading in my journal that I looked around me and realized I had actually moved into an apartment with wooden floors where the morning sun was now warming my face. Other things had happened, but in a slightly different way. I had envisioned the date on which I left my old company to start my own practice, and I did leave my old company on that exact date, but for a different company.

Some things sounded too good to be true, but turned out to be even better in reality. I had been single for two years, and before traveling to California had just been on a few dates with a man who I hoped might be the Mr. Right I was looking for. It soon turned out he wasn't, but a month later I met the man who

Embracing the Future

AFFIRMATION: I step into the future with an open heart.

What is expected in life tends to be realized. If you anticipate an amazing, joyous, healthy, prosperous future, this is more likely to occur for you than if you assume the worst. Expect the best; be open for anything. Imagine your life filled with happiness.
Your wondrous future is resting on the horizon of your soul, shimmering and bright.

I am now sharing my life with. I didn't think it was possible, but the reality of this relationship surpasses everything I had dreamed of. There were also some things that didn't happen at all. I realized that was fine, that I no longer wanted them to happen, they had lost their importance to me.

I do this 'one year later' exercise regularly now, in different forms, to affirm where I want to be going in my life. Sometimes I do it with friends while enjoying a glass of wine. Sometimes I do it with my husband while we're on a hike, talking about the wonderful things that have happened to us both as individuals and as a couple. And sometimes I do it just by myself while journaling. Doing this enables me to check in with myself, to make sure I'm really doing what I want to be doing, that I'm moving forward, both in my personal life and in my business, into the direction I want to be going. Sometimes I think I want something, but when I imagine it's twelve months later and it has happened already, it doesn't really feel that juicy. That is when I know I'm not on the right track.

I don't have any special powers that help me to manifest things. I'm just like you, an ordinary person who is trying to live her best life possible. So what made the things on my dreamboard, and the experiences I had described to my friends during our 'one year later' evening, come true? I believe a big part of it is that these two tools helped me to get clear about what I really wanted my life to be like. Getting clarity about what you want is the first step to making it happen! Not knowing what you long for deep down inside is like getting into a car to just start driving without any idea of where you want to go. It might be fine for a while, but at some point you're going to want to have a sense of direction or you will feel quite lost.

Once you have an idea of where you want to go, you can ask yourself: "How can I get there?" You set the intention of reaching your destination, in this case the life you desire, and search for ways to help you reach it. In our car analogy, you would be looking at the map to see which routes are available, the shortest, the quickest or the most scenic route, and then decide which one you want to take. Once you are clear on your destination and have set your intention of reaching it, synchronicities will start happening.

I can't explain how or why it works, but I have experienced this over and over again. *Where intention goes, energy flows.* When you act as if things have already happened, your subconscious mind doesn't realize you are pretending and thinks this is the reality. Many Olympians who have won gold medals use this strategy of imagining their races countless times before the actual race, visualizing every detail hundreds of times; it's a well-known technique to help them improve and reach their goals. Imagining not just the end results but also your happy emotions makes it an even more powerful exercise. You are not only envisioning your future, but you are already feeling it!

Another reason I believe these tools work is that the act of sharing your dreams with others, as well as sharing in their dreams, can be incredibly emotionally empowering. You gather a tribe of supporters, people who believe in you and cheer you on. Everyone needs people like this in their life; they are the wind in your sails. Knowing that people are rooting for you gives you wings.

There are many ways in which you can gain a deeper understanding of who you are and what you truly want out of life and how you can make it happen. Creating a soul board can be a stepping stone from which you can continue. If you don't know what you want to do, imagine yourself one year ahead in the future and ask yourself: "What would I wish to have happened in the past year?" These two tools have proven to be invaluable to me, and I hope you may find them equally valuable.

Creating Your Soul Board

Don't ask yourself what the world needs;
ask yourself what makes you come alive. And then go and do that.
Because what the world needs is people who have come alive.

—HOWARD THURMAN

Want to make your own soul board, but not sure how to do it? Here are the steps:

Step one:
Take some deep breaths and go to that place of stillness inside you. Clear your head and meditate or just breathe for a few minutes. Connect to your intuition, your guides or your angels and ask for the messages you need to hear most at this time. Set the intention to be guided to the images that will help you uncover those messages.

Step two:
Collect images. Take notice of pictures, words and phrases that catch your attention or draw your eye. Don't judge, just cut them out. Whether you like the image or not is not important. You noticed it for a reason. Don't attach a meaning to it yet; that will come later. All you need to do at this stage is collect images that in one way or another touch you.

Step three:
Select the images that you will be using on your dreamboard. This is where the fun really begins! Start sifting through your pile of clippings and notice your reaction to each particular image. How does it make you feel? What pops into your mind when you look at it? Do you find it beautiful or are you just fascinated by it? Start putting images on your board, and see what it looks like, what it feels like.

Play with your images, move them around and notice what difference it makes. Remove some images and replace them with other images. How does that feel? Better? Lighter? Does the other image need to come back? You will intuitively know which images need to be there and which ones don't, and you will intuitively know in which place they need to go. Just pay attention to your feelings. Keep asking yourself "How does this feel? Does it feel better if I put this image next to this one or next to that other one?"

Take your time here, as this is where you are creating the magic. It is an organic process that allows your intuition to show you what you need to know. To me it's a form of modern day alchemy, as it transforms random images from magazines to messages from your soul. It's okay if you still have no clue which messages they are. I never know what will turn up on my board until it's finished. If you have images left over that don't find a place on your dreamboard this time, you can save them for your next board. I have cut out images that I didn't actually use until months or even years later, until the time was right for them to reveal their message.

Step four:
When you have finished your board, take a step back and look at it. What do you notice? Where is your eye drawn to immediately? There may be one image that feels like the center piece, even if it's not in the middle of your board. Do you see repetitions of feelings, objects, or phrases on your board? What is the overall theme of your board? Is there a certain color that is dominant? Do you see any symbolic representations? If you had to describe your board in just one word, what would it be? What is the feeling you get when looking at it? Is there a pattern that is becoming visible to you? Which messages do you get from it?

Put your board up in a place where you see it often. Take a picture of it and set it as the wallpaper on your computer or phone. Meditate on it. You might not be able to answer all of these questions straight away, but the more time you spend with it and look at it, the more insights you will get about what your soul is trying to tell you through these images. Some of the messages might be easy to see and others will be harder to unearth.

Step five:
Go deeper. Journaling about your board is a great way to decipher the messages your board holds for you, to connect with it on a deeper level. You might also show it to someone you fully trust and ask what they see. They may notice things that had escaped your attention so far. But remember that even though someone else might be able to offer interesting insights about your board, you are the only person who can feel whether they are true for you or not.

Your intuition speaks to you in symbols that mean something to you. For example, an image of a running horse might mean freedom to someone else, but if you fell off a horse when you were young, to you it might symbolize getting hurt or being afraid to fall or losing control. You are the expert on your soul board! And as with all things in life, the more you practice, the better you get at it, and that is definitely the case for getting to know your personal symbols.

Soul boards are wonderful for tapping into your intuition and finding out what it is you are really yearning for, but they are also one of the best ways to manifest things. At different times in my life, I have created abundance boards, creativity boards, relationship boards, even a 'theme for my year' board. For example, one year my word or theme for the year was 'adventure', so I created a board that represented what adventure meant to me, what it looked like and felt like, and put that up in a place where I could see it every day.

When you create a vision board with the intention to manifest more of something, pick images that represent how you want to feel rather than the material things you want to manifest. For example, if you want to create a soul board to invite more abundance into your life and a car is on top of your list of what you want to manifest, think about what feeling a car would give you rather than what type of car you would like. A car might feel like independence, freedom, adventure or having more time in your day to do the things you enjoy. Find images that reflect those feelings rather than the money you need to buy a car. A car is the solution you have imagined for your problem, but there may be many more possible solutions. By focusing on the end result you desire instead of how the issue should be solved, you open yourself up to other solutions that you might have never thought of.

When I was preparing to start my own coaching practice, I made soul boards to gain clarity and insight into the soul of my business. By intuitively collecting images, I connected with the big vision I was holding for my business, with my ideal clients, with the services I wanted to offer. It helped me to brand my business and get clear on my marketing messages. You can do the same thing for your business, your career, your home, or anything else you want to get clarity about.

Creating soul boards and feeling what it would be like if things had already happened has felt like inviting my future. And I haven't invited just any future, but the future I wanted the most. You can do the same thing. The tools I have described to create a life I love are both powerful and empowering, and they will work for you too. You can proactively create your future instead of seeing what happens while you just go along with what life seems to have in store for you. You can beckon the life of your dreams and welcome it with open arms, holding the door wide open. When you know what you want, which values are the most important in your life, what you truly desire deep down inside you, you will find the answers to how to manifest it. Be open and have faith. Believe, both in yourself and in the magic that can happen when you are really committing to yourself. Pay attention to synchronicities and opportunities and take action. Not only are you ready to live a life that you love, you are worthy of it. And when you do, you help make this world a happier place.

∽

Bibliography
Coelho, Paulo. *The Alchemist*. HarperCollins, 1993.

Healing the Past

*AFFIRMATION: I step into my future
with strength and clarity.*

*Your past (and even your past lives)
affects your present. A powerful
healing is occurring for you right
now. Beneath the surface, there are
forces dissolving old blockages and
limitations. This has a positive effect
on every aspect of your life, including
your health, your relationships,
and even your creativity.*

LAURIE LARSON
Bismarck, North Dakota, USA

IT WAS AFTER enrolling in a Philosophy of World Religions class in college, and hungering to learn more, that Laurie realized she was a seeker. Though she has always had an inner knowing, that class became the defining moment that began her conscious spiritual journey.

Born in Korea, Laurie was adopted as a child and grew up in the Midwest of the United States. She has lived in many states as well as Mexico, Japan and Germany. Laurie has worked in various fields of politics, business, human services, banking, and education, with a focus on starting new projects and programs. She has also owned and managed two small businesses.

Along with being a Certified Soul Coach and Past Life Coach, Laurie has trained in Hypnotherapy, Reiki, Space Clearing, Clutter Clearing, A.R.E. Studies, Landmark Education, Spiritual Directorship, Resiliency, Akashic Records, and Abraham-Hicks.

Her greatest joy is working with people to help them find and express their true passion. She firmly believes that each of us has our own innate wisdom within and sees her role as being present so that you can fully realize and appreciate YOUR magnificence, and the immense joy that is available for you. You can contact her at www.pathwaysofawareness.com to schedule an appointment.

Everyone Has a Story to Tell

LAURIE BRYAN LARSON

When we accept and live in the great flow of life, we don't
know the whole story. But we can put one foot in front of the
other and trust that we are where we're meant to be.

I now see that my journey to Soul Coaching began long ago, but officially manifested itself in the year 2007. I had decided to create a practice where I could work with people to assist them in becoming whole and authentic. I wanted to incorporate all the knowledge that I had accumulated on my own spiritual journey, which formally began during the summer of 1972 when I took a class in the philosophy of Eastern Religions in college. It was the first time that I had actually initiated reading outside of the prescribed class curriculum. This particular class excited me so much that a spark was ignited within me. Truth be told, I was in summer school because I was working to pay off a loan to my friend, the Dean of Women. She had loaned me money earlier in the year for an abortion.

So, from that class, I began to question: what is my purpose? I remember feeling or wishing that I could be more like those people who seemed so sure of what they were meant to do in this lifetime. Those who become engineers, artists, teachers or truck drivers, have a visible skill. I felt as though my abilities weren't so visible. Although my talents were not any less than that of say a brain surgeon, like so many people, I did not see the uniqueness that was me. My talents lay in the heart. I wanted to be able to say or express them, to be able to say, "This is who I am and this is what I do."

I had been adopted from Korea when I was almost 6 years old by an American family. Over the years, I discovered that I had two brothers who shared the same birth mother as me. Frank was a baby when I left Korea for the United States, and Patrick had yet to be born. Through synchronicity, when my birth mom passed on in 1985, my brother Patrick had discovered a letter that I had written to our birth mom, expressing that I did not wish to reestablish a relationship with her. He also found my adoptive mother's phone number in our mom's personal effects and called my adoptive mother to let her know that our biological mom had passed.

I imagine that he spoke with her because his father had passed on by this time as well, and his relationship with our other brother was fractured. But having read my letter, he let my adoptive mother know, on no uncertain terms, what he thought about me.

To her credit, my adoptive mother encouraged him to understand that he and I had experienced different things in life, and that my not desiring to reestablish a relationship with my birth mom was a result of that. She asked him if he would give his contact information to her, knowing that I might want to reach out to him, if that was agreeable with him. And it was.

Synchronicity occurred again. I was living in Japan at the time, as my then husband was in the United States Air Force (USAF). Interestingly, Patrick was also in the USAF, but was in the process of getting out of the military to relocate to a town near Houston, Texas. We were preparing to depart Japan for our next duty station, San Antonio, Texas, three hours down the road from Houston. My then in-laws lived in Houston, along with several of my longtime friends.

Over the next couple of years, my husband traveled a lot because of his position in the Air Force, particularly overseas. Our sons were preschool age at the time and so on long weekends, I would pack them up into the car and we would go to Houston to visit their grandparents. On one of the early visits, I decided to call my brother Patrick. I dialed the number (yes, this was before cell phones) that Patrick had given to my adoptive mother. The number belonged to a family who had befriended Patrick through their son, who had been stationed with him in the Air Force. His friend's mother answered the phone and when I explained to her who I was, she said to me, "Oh, Patrick really needs you but I don't know if he will talk with you." I explained to her that I was going to be in Houston for the next couple of days and to please let Patrick know that I had called.

Within the next day or two, Patrick did return my call. Now remember, we had never 'met' in person, as he was born the year after I left Korea. Surprisingly, our phone conversation went really well and I suggested that perhaps we might meet in person so that we could continue to get to know one another better. Patrick agreed and I was able to have my sons' grandmother babysit them so that I was able to meet Patrick in person.

There was instant recognition on both of our parts when we met at a restaurant. This was a new experience for me, meeting and being with someone who had some of the same blood running through their veins as mine. We got caught up on what had transpired in each other's lives over dinner and I think we both found it amazingly easy to converse with one another. After dinner, Patrick wanted to show me his apartment. Perhaps we both wanted to hang on to the moment.

At his apartment, he showed me our mom's address book. Something told me at the time that I should ask for it but I didn't listen to that still small voice. The address book held the addresses of our Korean relatives, information that I didn't have. We ended our visit very congenially and we both had a desire to see one another again, preferably before the weekend ended. I told Patrick that I would see if I could make arrangements for us to get together again before my sons and I returned to San Antonio. When we hugged, I noticed that I could smell his body odor – a hint of things to come.

As it turned out, I could not see him again that weekend due to not being able to arrange babysitting for my sons. Knowing that Patrick was not yet ready to be introduced to his nephews, I called him to let him know that I would not be able to meet again on this trip, but that when I returned to San Antonio, I would call him to more fully explain. Only later did I realize that this would be the last time I would speak to or hear from Patrick for another twenty years. Unbeknownst to me, Patrick was in the beginning stages of schizophrenia.

When we met, Patrick had shared with me about the horrendous treatment that he and my other brother Frank had received from their father. There was unimaginable physical violence, culminating with their father placing them in foster homes in the United States and my mom in a mental hospital on the East Coast, so that he could return to the Philippines to be with his girlfriend.

Prior to our return to the United States from Japan, I had been in contact with my brother Frank. I had discovered, with assistance from a friend who was in Air Force personnel that Frank was also in the Air Force and was stationed at a base in the state of Delaware. He replied warmly to my initial letter and I decided to follow up with a phone call rather than a letter. Again, Frank was just a few months old when I left Korea. When I called his workplace, I eventually learned that Frank had been hospitalized at a military facility in South Carolina, with his first schizophrenic episode. I was able to locate his doctor, who told me that he would talk with Frank to see if he was interested in speaking with me.

Frank agreed and I'll never forget our first conversation. He was very highly medicated but the feeling again of having contact with a biological family member was something very unusual for me. While he was hospitalized, we spoke frequently on the phone and exchanged several letters. Frank indicated to me that he wanted to visit me and my family in San Antonio. But sadly, it never happened. I, of course, told him that I would come visit him whether he was in the hospital or when he returned to Delaware. But there never seemed like a good time with Frank for that to happen.

My then husband received orders for Germany in 1988, and even after our move overseas; Frank and I continued our correspondence, although the frequency lessened. He received a medical discharge, was attending college, had plans to marry, and then the letters stopped altogether in 1993.

Meanwhile, I continued to send Patrick correspondence a couple of times a year to a halfway house address in Central Texas that I had tracked down. I wanted him to know that I was there for him, should he want to reach out. One day in the 1990's, I received one of the letters back saying that it was no longer forwardable. I made many attempts to locate him over the intervening years. Of course, the Internet wasn't available in those early years or as readily as it is now, so I used what contacts I had to assist me in my search. Because of privacy laws, it was nearly impossible to receive any information.

By 2007, I had developed a strong desire to coach people to become their authentic selves, but I also wanted it to be on a deeper level than life coaching. I wanted the focus to be on a soul level. I had already chosen the name of my practice – *Soul Coaching*. But, before I hung out my shingle and started my Soul Coaching practice, I felt I should first investigate to see if anyone else was using that name. This idea came to me through having been a small business owner previously. I now know that it was guidance, my inner knowing, that led me to the computer to search that day. Sure enough, in searching on the computer, I discovered that there was a Soul Coaching program, and the purpose was very similar to what I had been considering offering. Imagine my surprise when I discovered this! As Denise Linn, the creator of Soul Coaching says, "There are no accidents!"

Not wanting to reinvent the wheel, I printed out the program description from Denise's website realizing that this was something I wanted to pursue. I knew by then that the Universe speaks to us so clearly; we just need to listen. But then, don't you know, life happened, as it so often does.

During this time, I was also looking at a genealogy research site and typed in my birth mom's name. Up popped my brother Frank's name, showing that he had passed on in 1995 in Colorado. That was the first time that I was aware of his passing.

In my trying to find out what happened to Frank, as he would have been 36 years old at the time of his passing, I discovered that he had taken his own life in a park in Colorado. When I received what few possessions that were found on him, primarily his identification cards, the ravages that the illness had imparted on him became cruelly apparent. A photo ID, taken just a couple of months before his suicide, showed a very sad Frank. That picture spoke volumes to me. In a couple of other photos taken earlier, he had been so vital and full of life.

In researching Frank's death, I also discovered that he had left some money in a savings account. What this required was that I locate my brother Patrick, as we would share the money by law. I went into detective mode to find Patrick, but this time, I had the advantage of the Internet. It seemed as though Patrick had continued to spend many of the most recent years in Central Texas. A work contact, whose husband was on the staff of a Congressman in Central Texas, checked the rolls of the local Veterans Hospital and discovered that Patrick had been treated there in the previous year.

I took a chance and called the hospital to see if Patrick might currently be hospitalized there, or if someone might know his whereabouts. I was put in touch with the woman who ended up being Patrick's case worker. She told me that he was living in a half-way house in a nearby town and that she would place a call to him to see if he was willing to talk with me. Clearly, besides him needing to know about Frank's passing and financial legacy, I was interested in reconnecting with him as well.

Patrick agreed to talk with me, and after a few conversations and letters, I decided to fly down to Texas from Washington, DC, for a reunion. Patrick was in a residential program at the Veterans' hospital that focused on life skills, so that he could live independently. He had essentially been living on the street for the previous 20 years, which is sadly not uncommon among people who have a mental illness, even today. Our reunion went well, and throughout 2007 we visited each other on a regular basis, culminating with us spending Christmas together in Washington, DC, in 2007, where he experienced a schizophrenic episode. The episode was a shocking reminder to me about his true condition.

I had put off attending the Soul Coaching certification for at least a year, due to the reunion with my brother. I'd also been considering going back to graduate school to receive a Master's in Social Work,

> ### Being in the Flow
>
> AFFIRMATION: *I am in the flow of the universe.*
>
> *Everything is falling into place because you aren't resisting the drift of the great river of life. Let go of the shore and allow the currents to dictate your direction. You don't need to decide and plan everything yourself. Let things flow effortlessly.*

which would allow me to work independently as a Soul Coach, while my clients could claim my services on their insurance. But when I enlisted the support of a career counselor in January of 2008, she encouraged me to forego the graduate training as she could see that it was Soul Coaching that really juiced me. That day, when I came home from work, I applied online to attend the Soul Coaching certification course being offered in May.

Since my finances were limited – I was still paying off debt from my divorce – I was clearly in need of assistance with the tuition. I wrote up an email to my friends and family, telling them about Soul Coaching, my desire to attend the course, and asking for their financial support, and if they weren't able to support me financially, to support me in their thoughts, prayers and meditations. I also said that if they contributed $100 or more that I would provide them a free session upon my return. The response was tremendous! I had a down payment for the course due in March – 6 weeks from the time I sent my email – and I received enough in contributions to make that down payment.

In May of 2008, I flew from Washington, DC, to San Luis Obispo, California. The next day, a group of us were picked up at the hotel by Denise and her husband David. Interestingly, for the nine days of our training, all of us in the car ended up being roommates in the Buddha Room, aptly named for the Buddha statue that lay in repose over the fireplace. We, in the Buddha room, would wake up in the morning, stumble out and put on the hot water for tea and make a pot of coffee. We began the day in each other's company, often giving each other card readings from the plethora of cards that Denise offered, or discussing an important dream that one of us had recalled. The only incident in the room occurred with a mouse. And if you want to see grown women standing on their beds making screeching noises, just introduce a mouse into the room!

We ate family style meals and we set the table for each meal from the sumptuous collection of linens and dishes that Denise offered. Each seemed to carry a theme and was dependent on the people who were setting the table. So every meal was indeed a celebration – visually, nutritionally and for the soul. The most unforgettable thing for me was the absolute joy we experienced there. It was a veritable feast for the eyes, body, and soul. Our group called themselves the *Joytribe*!

From the moment we arrived, with the welcome gifts of aromatherapy spray, Soul Coaching oracle cards, Denise's Space Clearing book, book bag, water bottle with each person's name inscribed, and including socks – yes, it sometimes gets cold in the summer in California – one had the sense that great forethought had gone into making sure that we felt welcomed, as well as it being good modeling for us as future Soul Coaches. For me, the highlights include lifelong friendships with an international group of sixteen people, with some of whom I've enjoyed multiple reunions.

Connection is an important component of Soul Coaching, primarily connecting with that special place within each of us so that we can be the glorious creatures that we truly are and thereby facilitating those soul connections with others. Was it all sublime? – no – but I think that anyone who is on a path of greater self-awareness realizes that such intensity may bring out the 'stuff' that needs to be dealt with.

We worked through the entire Soul Coaching curriculum, so that when we offered the 28 day program to others after the completion of the course, we would be intimately familiar with it. As I reflect back on that time, it really was a perfect way for us to learn the Soul Coaching curriculum – from large group discussions and presentations to smaller groups for learning about Soul Journeys. We also spent time working on all the exercises that are offered in the program, be it a timeline of our life, a spirit stick or a collage. And after we left the retreat, together as a group we repeated the 28 day program that is the core of Soul Coaching, complete with a Quest at the end. I chose to do my quest on the banks of the Potomac River, across from the Lincoln Monument in Washington, DC.

So, for me, the memories of becoming a Soul Coach have to do with the sights, sounds – all the sensory experiences – the feelings. This, to me, is the essence of Soul Coaching. It's the peeling away of the layers until what is left is our core; and how we best access that is through our senses. When I went back to my life, I was in a different place inwardly. I finally left a job that was sucking me dry of the very essence of who I am. Why did it take me so long? A benefit of Soul Coaching is that my 'beating myself up' over that has been minimal. One of the things that I love about Denise as a teacher is that the growth that she encourages is totally nonjudgmental. There is no 'should' or 'have to'. There is so much to learn from accepting ourselves exactly where we are. When we accept and live in the great flow of life, we don't know the whole story. We can't. But we can put one foot in front of the other and TRUST; trust that we are where we are meant to be, and trust that all is OK.

Soul Coaching encourages us to be our authentic selves. We each have the wisdom within to know what is best for us in every situation. Often, it is just a matter of tapping into that inner knowing and allowing our authentic selves to shine forth. In so many cases, through life's disappointments and challenges, we have allowed our inner brilliance to become dulled, perhaps even unrecognizable.

I believe that everyone has a story to tell. We each bring a unique point of view, and it is important to fully express it in a way that is of benefit to ourselves, as well as to others. Maybe, in some way, my story has touched something in you; perhaps ignited an ember of recognition that your own story is just as important as anyone else's.

Yes, I am ordinary, but some extraordinary things have occurred in my life. May you be inspired to peel away the layers to allow your beautiful spirit, that part that is uniquely you, to shine forth, because you already ARE amazing! And that is what Soul Coaching is all about. It has a beautiful way of encouraging everybody to recognize their value by just being their authentic selves.

Everyday Spirituality

> *At the center of your being you have the answer;*
> *you know who you are and you know what you want.*
>
> —LAO TZU

It is my belief that what we do every day is important for our development. Towards that end, I'm going to include some of my favorite daily routines that help to keep me balanced and on my spiritual path. Do I do them every day? Let's be honest. No, I don't do them every day. However, I do them most days, which is the key. If I slack, I can tell because I'm grumpier and generally feel off-kilter. For me, balance is the key.

So, in the morning, upon rising, I will focus on the most recent soul collage that I've made. I look at every picture and word that is on my collage, inhaling the feeling behind each image or phrase as a reminder of the intention that I set for this collage when I made it. I then look at a daily calendar that contains an affirmation, to set the tone for my day and as a reminder about a particular positive focus for that day. Next, I open up my email and read an inspirational quote that is sent to me electronically every day from one of my favorite websites that focuses on gratitude. And if need be, I will look at a couple of other emails from other positive sources. This all helps me to set my intention for the day, which generally focuses on *being* love. This daily routine keeps me mindful of loving both myself and others.

On some of those more challenging days, if I find myself in my head more than in my heart, I will take three deep inhalations and exhalations. Just doing this simple time out is truly effective. Try it the next time you're feeling a bit anxious!

At the end of the day, I read passages from two or three books that focus on spirituality and personal growth. I find this a perfect way for me to put the day behind me and to imbue my sleep with positive energy.

There are many other practices that I incorporate throughout the day, again depending on what I'm feeling on a soul level – be it walking, using aromatherapy sprays, lighting candles or pulling a card from an oracle deck.

However, the practice that really juices me is taking photographs! Although I've always loved photography and took a class many years ago, I think I felt somewhat deficient as a photographer. Interestingly, one of my classmates in Soul Coaching took many pictures during our time together and that piqued my interest.

This time I approached photography with a different mindset. I 'listened' to that still small voice and when I saw something that really spoke to my soul, I snapped a picture on my cell phone. And I snapped without concern for, 'will it look good; will others like it?' I wanted to capture what my soul saw in that moment and by doing this, that's when the pictures spoke to others as well. Are all my pictures masterpieces? Hardly, but that's not important. And the less stellar pictures teach me as well, akin to the bumps we experience in life. Will my photography support me financially? Who knows? What I do know is that when I am taking pictures and allowing myself to truly be in the moment, it becomes a form of meditation for me. I am grateful for the ability to 'see' with my soul and to be able to capture those images.

Each of these practices works to keep me in balance on my spiritual path, and I know they can work for you as well. So, if you have a hobby or interest, I encourage you to approach it from your heart, and to see that when you create from the moment, it too can be a spiritual practice that feeds your new life story, the life of your dreams.

Proceeding Softly

*AFFIRMATION: My inner power
grows in moments of quietude.*

*Go forward, slowly and gently.
Stop to smell the daisies
and enjoy the view. Love and
appreciate what is here now.*

KYLA TUSTIN
Sydney, Australia

THE HEART AND soul of Kyla's life and her business, Your Power Centre, include what matters most to her: Truth, Passion, Freedom, Love, Creativity and awakening people to their light.

Her mission is to ignite your journey, ensuring it's fun and supports you to *Love Your Life* with confidence, as you clear the inner clutter, let go of past limitations, sabotaging beliefs, and step into your *light* – living a life aligned with what matters most to you.

Kyla integrates her work as a Soul Coach, Confidence Coach, Certified Angel Intuitive™, Advanced Integrated Energy Therapist®, Crystal Energy Therapist® and Essence of Angels® practitioner, to step you out of the stresses of daily life and into the calm – feeling safe to journey to your Soul and beyond, where you'll find the answers you seek and unveil your True Self with an inspired sense of purpose, passion and energy for life.

Kyla offers one on one sessions and group workshops for adults, corporate businesses, children and teenagers. Her authentic style of teaching is direct from the heart. She shares the stories and mishaps of her own life and provides you with practical tips and resources for living an everyday spiritual and mindful life.

Kyla runs her practice from two locations in Sydney's North and also provides online programs and sessions for clients living outside Sydney and Australia via Skype, email and telephone.

To join Kyla's powerful community of everyday spiritual souls embracing their light, visit her at www.yourpowercentre.com.au

Awakening Our Light

KYLA TUSTIN

Once I trusted enough to let go, to open my heart and listen,
the beauty and light in my life unfolded and all the doors began to open.

I wear a mask and it protects me. It protects me from being seen, from being hurt and from living exposed in a world where I feel different. This mask becomes me and owns me and though its protection feels so safe, it is time to remove it. It's time for me to step out into the world as me, as my light. It is time to acknowledge my gifts and the parts of me I have left hidden from myself and the world – my natural ability to feel what others feel, to see beyond our physical world, and to know that I am so blessed to support myself and others to release our old stories, our wounds and our pain, and to ignite our lives, so we may create a community and a world filled with heart and soul.

Feeling different

After much soul-searching over the years, I am able to pinpoint choices and experiences that have led me to put on my mask, to disassociate from my self, to stop listening to the wisdom of my soul, to try to 'fit in' instead, and to choose fear over love. One meaningful moment was leaving behind my much-loved grandparents at a very young age, as we moved between New Zealand, Hong Kong and Australia. I began to believe that I never really had my place, a place where I felt I belonged. This belief led to future moments, which fueled my fear of being 'different', including being bullied in the early years of school. Though I knew I never quite fitted in to the world around me, all I ever wanted was to be like everyone else. To protect myself from a very young age, and to cope with my high sensitivity towards the spiritual world, my own feelings and those of others, I chose to shut down my tele-empathic feelings and senses. What I didn't know was that these choices would mean spending my adolescent life feeling totally disconnected to everything and everyone, constantly trying to prove my self-worth and find my own truth.

As a teenager, I didn't understand that I needed to take full responsibility for my choices. So if I did something that I wished I hadn't, which usually involved getting drunk, I would either make jokes about it or hide from it completely. I now know that deep down below the protective barriers, a part of me was trying to avoid feeling the shame. It wasn't until I hurt someone I really cared for with these lies that I was able to truly feel and see the pain I had created by trying to hide my actions. It was after this experience that I learnt the value of *truth* and that lies only create even greater self-deception and hurt. I was able to understand that everyone deserves the truth so that they can make choices based on this and not have this power of choice taken away. I made a commitment to myself from that point forward, I would start making much more responsible choices and never lie or step away from my truth again. My spirit and soul have definitely kept me to this promise.

For years the lies, alcohol, drugs and emptiness within kept me isolated from my deep wounds, though I longed for acceptance. My inward journey has shown me how my early years were spent avoiding the present, my heart, and my self. Avoidance was the only life I knew. I had chosen to play it safe, to avoid having feelings or being vulnerable at any cost, and to follow the rules (though this never quite happened). So I grew up believing I was limited in my potential, that I was never really good at anything, feeling worthless. I constantly strove to do everything perfectly, holding on at all costs, never wanting to make a mistake, and never ever letting anyone know, even myself, how I really felt inside behind this mask.

Waking Up
Thankfully, in my mid-twenties I began to very slowly wake up from the masquerade I had created. As I began to question my life, I was faced with the realization that some of my friends and my goal of fitting in to the norm were slowly slipping away. I was learning to understand that the reason I didn't fit in was that I'd never allowed myself to understand 'who I was'. The endless nights partying with friends no longer masked the void within me, and the days to follow those nights seemed to leave much more than the pain of a sore head. My lonely heart ached to truly feel love, to be forgiven for the hurt I felt had caused myself and others, and to embrace my hidden gifts, to create a life that finally made sense.

To the outside world I was confident, successful, and knew exactly what I wanted out of life. The amazing thing about my mask is that the more I practiced wearing it, the better I became at this deception, so that even I believed that this was 'me'. Having worked in successful corporate roles for many years, I had a great job, great salary, a loving and supportive partner and a beautiful apartment in Sydney. My life appeared enviable...

But inside I started to question if this was all there was to life. I began to understand that something was missing, and that something was *me*. I would ask myself on those dark nights – was it really me that wanted this high paying role, long hours at work, and who dreamed of becoming a CEO of a multi-million dollar business? Or was this hectic life I had created merely to mask what was really going on inside: the fear of stepping outside, being different from everyone else and potentially not being liked or accepted? I was afraid of being vulnerable enough to ask, and listen, for what my heart truly desired: freedom, passion, and shining my inner light for all to see.

At this time I was blessed to have been working with an amazing intuitive counselor and a crystal healer. Both of these wonderful women supported me during this transformative time. They encouraged me to acknowledge the wounds I had previously refused to feel, yet still held deep inside. The more I allowed myself to feel, the more I realized how dissatisfying parts of my life were, and how I continually chose to run away from the conflict within. My life had been a well-planned project based on a lot of hard work but not much depth.

I discovered that I could look past my story and reconnect with the real me. For the first time in my life, I began to allow myself to heal by fully feeling what and how I felt, and making choices that felt right in my heart, not just my head. I made new choices not because everyone else said it was a good idea but because I heard a gentle calling inside that simply felt right. And as I woke up, I started to understand how disconnected from myself, my heart, my dreams and my soul's journey I had become.

This feeling of disconnection led me to enroll in a two-year intuitive development course, recommended to me by my intuitive counselor. I knew very little about this course, and even less about where it was leading me. In hindsight, this was probably a good thing or my ego and mind might have come up with even more excuses than it did not to enroll. I felt I was being guided to join this class, and so I chose to listen. As I entered the classroom that first night, I knew I had arrived somewhere special and my life would never be the same again.

I know now that this class was a clear message sent from my soul, and that it provided me with the support I needed to really ignite my inward journey and open up to my intuitive gifts and healing abilities. It allowed me to acknowledge all the different parts of me, including the parts of my past I had hidden from sight all my life for the fear of being judged. The discoveries I made in this class would lead me to choose to leave my old life behind, to give up my highly-paid banking career, and for my partner and I to leave our beautiful home in Sydney's Double Bay to adventure the world once more, this time with open eyes.

As we decided to pack up our lives for our trip, people around us commented on how courageous this was, but in my heart and soul I knew I had no choice. I could stay on the path I knew, which felt comfortable but unsatisfying, or I could finally journey within to the unknown, which though it contained some fear, I knew I just had to embrace. Once I trusted enough to let go, to open my heart and listen, the beauty and light in my life unfolded and all the doors began to open. Within a short time of planning our trip, we had rented out our furnished apartment, my partner was given the time off work, and I had found a replacement for my work role. Our choices were fully supported with ease and grace. All I had to do was be willing to open that first door and look within. Now if I feel fear when I'm following my heart, I know that I can choose to continue on my own path anyway, knowing that the fear only proves how important it is to move forward, and that my nervousness is actually my excitement buzzing within.

Our journey took us to many amazing places. We relaxed in beach bungalows and tree houses in Thailand, trekked to Everest Base Camp, volunteered in the Himalayas in Kashmir and relished in the luxuries of Europe. Our adventure across the USA enabled me to discover even more about crystals and energy healing and to study with Denise Linn to become a Certified Soul Coach. Nonetheless, the most important part of this whole exploration was the opportunity to take the time to journey within, to begin to really find myself again and to feel the love and joy that shone within my heart.

The Power of 'Doing Nothing'

Through this journey I was to discover where in my life I have allowed my mind, my ego, my limiting beliefs and my self-imposed identity to rule me. Wanting to be perfect, to control everything and always keeping busy were highly effective ways for me to avoid 'being'. I would distract myself with work, study, other people's lives, email, television and the internet. However, as I stepped out of the safety of my life and into a year of very little plans – even less 'to do's' and adventures where I couldn't control a thing – I began to understand how these distractions kept me away from my stillness, preventing me from listening to my inner wisdom.

The easiest way to listen to this inner wisdom is to become still. When Denise Linn introduced the 'doing nothing' exercise to me in our Soul Coaching training, I found it difficult at first to understand the instructions and asked endless questions like "Can I read a book in my 'do nothing' hour; can I meditate; can I walk; can I play music?" And with each question I received the same response "Doing nothing, means absolutely nothing."

I was finally satisfied when Denise advised me that it was OK for me to do nothing in a tranquil place in nature. But I still couldn't quite understand why this exercise was such a foreign concept to me. There must have been a time recently when I sat contentedly and did nothing... It soon become clear that I didn't even have a memory of the last time I relaxed, let alone did nothing. Even my most enjoyable forms of relaxation, like yoga and meditation, were always spent 'trying'.

Stepping into Stillness

AFFIRMATION: *My power is born in the majesty of silence.*

Take a moment to enter into the silent, deep place within you. Be still. Let everything go, and focus on what is truly important. Imagine spiraling down into the source of your essence. Breathe deeply. Allow your body to relax into the present moment, the here-and-now.

I was never really satisfied with just being me because I didn't quite know who this was. So, choosing to spend quiet time 'being' with my self was quite a scary thought.

I began to truly comprehend the power I had handed over to the distractions in my life. Being busy kept me safe because it stopped me from feeling. As I reviewed past turning points in my life, I came face to face with this pattern of busyness. When I looked back to a tragedy which had occurred within my family, I realized the 'busyness pattern' had led me to stay at work, to try to figure out what practical steps I could take to help out, but to keep working. In trying to keep control and avoid feeling too much, I had missed out on what I desired the most: the miracle of connection by sharing my truth and my feelings, and allowing myself and others to really know 'me'. I had created a safe way of coping with stress and traumatic situations – and that was to keep going, to avoid stopping and never talk about, let alone allow myself to feel how I felt. It am still quite amazed that one of my greatest lessons on my journey, after years of busily working and studying, would be to learn to 'do nothing', to simply *be*.

Surprisingly, 'doing nothing' required a lot of discipline and commitment on my part as I faced the noises in my life and chose to honor myself, to 'be with my self'. Now I feel joy at the thought. There are still days when I notice old patterns sneaking in, when I tell myself that I am too busy to stop, or to do the activities that bring me the most satisfaction and joy. When this happens, I stop and ask myself "What am I trying to avoid today?" The wisdom, miracles and answers are always right in front of me, as long as I stop long enough to listen.

The miracle of listening to my heart

My journey has taught me that miracles are not just in the big 'Aha Moments' of life, but also all the small daily experiences which fill my heart with immense love and joy, like the butterfly gliding in the wind, dancing uninhibited under a full moon, or watching a proud mother playing with her child in the park. I used to miss these heart moments because I spent so much time 'in my head' contemplating questions like: "How can I earn more money, become better at everything, be a perfect partner, friend, student, and achieve all the goals I set myself?" The consequence was that I continually missed out on the most important time in my life, and the most important person to be living it with. And that time is *now* and the person is *me!*

> *Yesterday is history, tomorrow is a mystery, and*
> *today is a gift; that's why they call it the present.*

Recently, I was running through the nearby national park when a voice in my head began to shout "You don't have time for this run. You have things to do!" There it was again, trying to tell me to *do* instead of *be*. This time I caught myself out, and chose to ignore this nagging voice. I followed my intuition down a longer path I hadn't taken before. As I ran a little further, just to show my ego who was boss, I found myself at a beautiful cliff. Looking out at sea, I caught sight of an amazing pod of dolphins jumping and playing. So I took time out to sit down and enjoy this beautiful scene, thanking the universe for this wondrous opportunity to grow. This reminded me once again just how wonderful life can be when I follow my heart, and what miraculous experiences I can miss out on when I let my ego and mind take over. Though my ego is useful in keeping me motivated and driven, its loud voice has the power to take over and prevent me from being in the authentic flow of my life and relationships.

In every moment I have a choice to move forward in the direction my heart and soul is calling me. So I choose to remind myself each day of the importance of slowing down, not taking too much on, setting clear boundaries, finding balance in my life, and always making time for myself, my passions, my joys and my loved ones. Will there be mystical dolphins at the end of the path? I don't know, but it is always worth finding out, and along the way, enjoying the journey. Whichever moments I allow myself to experience in my days are always up to me; I just need to ensure that I prioritize myself into my day. The best part about following the flow of my heart on the day I saw the dolphins was that I planted a seed for the rest of that day. I ended up achieving more and with much greater pleasure because I let go of the need to control and resist!

Accepting My Self

Acceptance is a sacred act of power. Accept your light!

—DENISE LINN

I now agree wholeheartedly with the well-known phrase: "What you resist persists." When feelings of sadness, anger or a sense of being overwhelmed arrive in my days, I can now see they bring a gift which requires acknowledgement and review. They are neither good nor bad; they just awaken me to an imbalance which I need to explore, not ignore.

My daily path of self-acceptance is sometimes one of the toughest journeys in my life. But the gifts far surpass the challenges, as in every moment I have the opportunity to recognize the signs and to choose to let go, to step out of fear, and embrace balance and love through my thoughts, feelings and actions. The more I truly accept every part of who I am and the lessons, gifts and growth I receive in my life, without the need to compare, be right, control and judge, the easier my life continues to be, and the more free I feel I am to live and dream as me.

We do not remember days... we remember moments.

—CESARE PAVESE

With fresh eyes and balance in my life, I can see the value in embracing some of those life lessons at an early age. Each has led me to the true *me*, igniting my spiritual self and embracing my 'I Am'. They have led me to become a teacher and mentor to support others to open the door and find themselves again. My journey has taught me that there really are no mistakes in life. Each lesson teaches me to look within and to unveil a deeper part of me so that I might find a wonderful new understanding and gift which I can share with the world. My journey is never over; there really is no perfection, and no goal that can be attained which will satisfy my ego's burning desire to achieve. There are simply many moments of 'being', with miracles within these moments for me to discover even more about my self.

My journey to unmask Kyla and introduce her to the world continues to be exciting, amazing, and sometimes painful, and I wouldn't change a minute of it! There will always be adventures to embark on, mountains to climb, history to resolve, obstacles to move and decisions on which path to take. But one thing I know for sure is that even in moments of doubt, if I choose to follow my heart, and to let go of the noise, there is always a helping hand from above, willing to support and guide me so that even the mountains don't seem so big. All I have to do is provide the stillness for my messages and guidance to come through.

I am grateful for the teachings my journey brings me every day, and am blessed to be able share this amazing journey back to self with you, as you embark on your own self-discovery and find your own safe and sacred place to go within. This journey to ignite your heart and soul, allows you to effortlessly and uncondition-ally love and accept yourself, and open the door to your greatest potential – You!

I believe that as each of us ignites our own power within, filled with confi-dence, compassion, courage and an awakened commitment to our true spiritual self, we awaken many more on this earth to understanding the great value there is in making ourselves, our joy, our hearts and our truth a priority in our lives. So I invite you now to remove your mask, and continue your journey to awaken your true self, as you create your own recipe to ignite your life and most importantly, enjoy the miracles along the way!

A Recipe to Ignite Your Power Centre – YOU!
Ingredients
* *You*
* *Your Joy*
* *Your Passion*
* *Your Stillness*

Method
Step One:
Add a drop of *You* into everything you do today. If you want to laugh, laugh. If you want to cry, cry. If you want to sing, sing. Step into your truth and express yourself in every moment through the way you dress, talk, listen and love. And as you do, open up your heart to allow your light to shine out into the world. Write up a list

of your top ten values e.g. truth, love, family, passion, freedom. Your values are the most important things in your life. Then ensure that every choice you make aligns with these values.

Step Two:
Sprinkle *Your Joy* into your miracle moments today. As Denise says "Joy is your natural birthright." Say "Yes" to life today, and choose to embrace your moments as an opportunity to sprinkle your joy into the world. Create a Joy Journal and fill it creatively each day with at least three memories of all the wonderful experiences of joy you have had today. eg. the synchronicities, coincidences, new experiences, meaningful people you've met, and the moments which made your heart sing. Journal about each and every little miracle that occurred in your life today; hopefully there will be lots more than three. Then, include a description outlining what in these things invoked joy within you.

Step Three:
Stir in *Your Passion*. Feel it in your heart, and ask yourself exactly what it is that brings you great feelings of joy and love. Then do or be it! Let nothing, not even your ego, stop you from enjoying or becoming your passion. To identify your passion, begin by asking yourself what brings a smile to your face and warms your heart. What did you love to do as a child; what could you talk about for days; what do you do that is just for you; or if you were handed 10 million dollars what would you spend your time doing or being?

Then, as well as following your passions, choose to live every miracle moment and experience in your life with passion. You may choose to sit in your car in traffic with passion by turning up the music and singing out loud, or start a friendly conversation with someone in the elevator, or simply choose to smile at every person you encounter today. The choice is yours, so choose whatever steps feel right for you to find passion in all of your daily moments.

Step Four:
Combine all other ingredients with time for *Your Stillness*. Every day, allow yourself 10 to 15 minutes of stillness and silence to 'do nothing', as you sit with your breath and your heart beat. Be a sacred observer of your life, and allow the gifts of your thoughts and emotions from your day to rise to the surface to be released. For a double dose of stillness, once a week, schedule in one whole hour of 'doing nothing' time. Remember, doing nothing means absolutely no distractions. That's right: no iPhone, no books, no music, no television, no walking, and you can't even meditate.

One of my passions is crystals, so here is an added ingredient you might like to add to your daily blend...

Added Energy Boost – A Crystal Friend

I personally like to bring a special crystal friend with me every day, either in my pocket, my bag, at my desk, on a necklace or bracelet, or by taking along my crystal vibrational essence sprays. Experiment with what works best for you. As powerful energy conductors, each crystal holds within it a unique energy vibration which, when integrated with your pure intention, amplifies to support the release, rebalancing and realignment of your energy bodies to support your journey back to self.

∽

BERNIE GIGGINS
Karalee, Queensland, Australia

BERNIE GIGGINS HAS a wealth of metaphysical knowledge and experience, extending from personal heartache to professional development. She is able to connect on a Soul level with her clients, and uses many ancient techniques to provide freedom from emotional trauma through her personal sessions.

Bernie's extensive energetic qualifications include training with Denise Linn to become a Certified Soul Coach and Past Life Regression Coach, as well as training under mentors Brandon Bays and Kevin Billett as a Practitioner of international The Journey™. She has Practitioner and Certifications in Dowsing, Reiki Master, Crystal Bed Energy Healing, Visionary Intuitive Healing, Ear Candling, Indian Head Massage, and loves using Young Living oils in her practice.

Bernie is known as the 'wounded inner child whisperer' clearing many traumatized souls of their past subconscious programming and back into conscious living in the present moment with amazing results. She prides herself in being able to access the deep subconscious mind where the wounded child resides, giving the child a voice which in turn gives the adult another chance and choice for transformational changes to take place.

Bernie teaches in an organic way, honoring and respecting each soul's unique journey. Her workshops empower and inspire her clients, providing the change they thirst for, and she continually helps other souls to find their calling and to live the life of their dreams through her 'Soul Synergy Centre'.

Bernie loves relaxing with her husband, children and grandchildren and enjoys life to the full. Contact her at Bernie's Innergetic Personal Soul Coaching www.innergeticpscoaching.com.au

Dream n'On Forever

BERNADETTE GIGGINS

*The Soul Journal is used to write Gratitude and Surrender entries –
the more grateful we are for what we have; the more we receive from the universe.*

*H*ave you ever wondered why you do things you never dreamt you would do? Have you repeatedly had dreams and visions about living in a different culture, and felt at home with people and cultures, vastly different from your own? In my childhood, I loved the Native American Indians, loved watching movies about them, and got upset when and if the soldiers hurt or cheated the Indians. I felt their pride and was inspired by them, as if I were one of them because they loved and respected the earth and the animals just like I did. I never understood this phenomenon as a child. Why did I feel so connected to them when I felt so alienated within my own family – who didn't understand me the way I felt the Indians would?

Decades later, I still had a strong yearning to finally meet and engage in conversation with Native American people. So, when I saw that a local intuitive counselor was sponsoring two American Indian Elders to come to our city for a talk, I immediately jumped at the chance to attend this awesome event. I felt as though I was with family!

After that meeting, I went to the library to look for books to borrow, opening my heart to any signs pointing to which book or author might have wisdom to share that would be beneficial for my higher self. A book titled *Soul Coaching, 28 days to discover your authentic self* by a Denise Linn popped up on the library computer screen. I thought to myself, "I don't have the time to sit for an hour each day and do this work," but I trusted that this was the book I was guided to. So respectfully, I took it home and started preparing what was needed for the next 28 days. Denise Linn's ancestry is Cherokee Indian, so I blessed her for this Native American link and also the universal guidance which drew me to this book at this time in my life. This book was to change my life forever.

I followed the guidance given in the book, the daily ritual Denise suggested, journal writing, noting what the universe was telling me, and really connecting myself to my creator, with no church between us, no lies and nothing kept hidden. In this program, you make a commitment to the universe and its creator to complete the course. There are four parts that you work through in a specific order: mental – air; emotional – water; spiritual – fire; and physical – earth. This process slowly strips away all of the uncomfortable past, uncovering who said what, how it felt, everything that is not authentic to you.

I had committed to waking up early, to use the early morning hours as my time for completing this program, before my children woke up, so that I could really focus on clearing the chains that were holding me back to the past. I remember so clearly on day 11 of mental – air week. Early that morning as I was writing my daily journal, my daughter came to me with a dream she had dreamt of the future. It was a very upsetting dream that held echoes of things that had not been healed from our family's past. In that moment, I had to find a voice of confidence and authority to reassure her in no uncertain terms that nothing like what she had dreamt would ever happen in this lifetime! I also knew in that moment, without a shadow of doubt, that the past can and would be healed. By working through the Soul Coaching book, I had discovered a new voice inside, one which now spoke with strength and love.

This was a turning point in my life, and after completing the Soul Coaching program, I knew I wanted to train with Denise Linn to become a Soul Coach – helping other souls to live the life of their dreams – to find their calling through clearing baggage that wasn't theirs, by guiding them back through their past lives to change their lives for the better.

After completing the Soul Coaching book, I tried to discover whether Denise Linn would be coming to Australia again so I could continue more courses with her. I felt utter dejection when I realized that the only way this could happen was if I traveled to see her in the USA. That night I dreamt, and really tried to imagine myself being on the plane, flying to her ranch and completing the course, feeling what it would be like.

Through the night, my ego kicked in and said "You can't go to America. You have school fees, a family to look after, etc." This plunged my mind, with my soul underneath, into despair. I felt I was back where I started, stuck in the same way of life, not able to escape. This was hard to face, after having tasted the freedom my soul yearned for. But my mind was only replaying the story of my life so far – childhood betrayals, being bullied as a child, almost getting to the top and someone else taking the glory, having the rug pulled out from beneath me, being told "You will be treated equally" only to have others given special treatment instead. This made me so upset, I continued crying, "Why can't I go to the USA to do Denise Linn's training and become a Soul Coach?' But my soul had other things I needed to learn yet, if only I could trust. Trust can be difficult for any adult who has had their trust betrayed as a child.

The next day there was a Mind, Body and Soul Expo, which was my outlet for spiritual guidance and healing, a gift I gave myself. While driving there I said, "If I can't go to America, then show me what else I am meant to do, thank you."

I met a wonderful Soul Coach called Maria Elita there who is also a Crystal Bed healer. Following my intuition, I had a couple of sessions with Maria, and then completed her practitioner course. Maria then introduced me to Scott Alexander King, the animal dreamer, who lived with shamans and sages around the world to learn the wisdom he shares today. Well, I thought, here is a shaman who has lived with Native Americans. Maybe I am to learn the way of the Australian Animal Dreaming? Meanwhile, I had not forgotten the commitment I had made back in June to attend Denise Linn's Soul Coaching training on her ranch in the USA. So, every morning when I walked my dog, I would stand in front of the sunrise and ask Grandfather Sun to guide my direction towards Denise's ranch, never giving up.

Then, three months later, my next door neighbor had to read a book, and needed someone who she could trust to be her guide and mentor as she was going through the process. This meant that I had to read the book as well. I told my friend that I really didn't have the time to do this, but she continued asking, and seemed so desperate, I felt obliged to read it. As it happened, I could not put the book down. *The Journey,* by Brandon Bays, was another book which took my body by the horns and allowed my soul to be free and to sing. Yes I helped my neighbor with her process, and with reiki and dowsing modalities, we got to the root cause of her issue and cleared it.

Brandon Bays stirred my soul, so I attended a beginner class and was blown away with what was released from the closets of my childhood held in my cellular memory bank. So I went to the next seminar of 'The Journey' in October 2008. Wow, I thought, here is another mentor who, like Denise Linn, also believes that "the soul loves the truth." The next seminar was even more powerful, uncovering more childhood scars and healing them on a soul level. I felt so alive, so free and liberated. I knew I needed to complete the Brandon Bay courses, and continue listening to my soul. I had still not forgotten Denise Linn, or my commitment to meeting her. I continued saying my morning prayer to be guided towards her. But it wasn't meant to be at this time. So I kept following the guidance of my soul, one step and one day at a time.

I noticed that here was an Abundance course of 'The Journey' coming up, in two weeks' time. But it was in Perth, on the western coast of Australia. I had never been to that side of the continent or flown that far before. If I wanted to complete 'The Journey' practitioner program now, I needed to do this course because there wasn't another one for at least six months. But I had never left my family before, I was still working full time, and where was I going to find the money or the time to travel, four days journey to and from? All these fears kept rising inside of me, but my soul's yearning was even greater. I knew I had to put my intentions out into the universe and trust that my family and I would be looked after. I was committed, so that's what I did. I told my husband, who possibly thought I was crazy, that I was going. I checked the flights and got the latest as it was the cheaper one; I got the time off work which was a little harder but I persisted, and I confidently asked 'The Journey Office' for a payment plan – all okay – so all systems go! Did I mention that I am extremely shy with strangers, a person of a few words unless it is something I am passionate about? But I kept following my soul's guidance, and everything was falling into place, easily.

The course produced amazing results. It uncovered more untruths about my identity and childhood wounds. How many more were there in my attic?

Over the next year, I was changing and blossoming into my own true self, still following my soul guidance. An old friend I hadn't seen for many years wanted to know if I had had a face lift, saying I looked so much younger and more vibrant! I told her "No, I just got rid of years of emotional baggage that wasn't mine!" In this next twelve months, I was guided to learn and follow the teachings of Florence Skovel Shinn through two of her books *Your Word is Your Wand* and *The Game of Life and How to Play it*. I was learning that you are what you say you are, and I now realize the energy behind what we think and speak. I am forever careful and now remind others that we have become lazy and take for granted what we say and do, not realizing the power of words and thoughts. Florence's teachings and affirmations also assist us in connecting our soul to the creator. Another powerful bible is *The Secret Language of the Body* by Inna Segal, which teaches that whatever you cannot express or clear can manifest into physical ailments.

Back to my Dream Goal of meeting Denise Linn... I had put this on the back burner as in my mind I had overspent on other courses, completing whatever else I needed to do. Yet I was still saying my intention every morning with my walk and leaving it up to the gods. My soul yearning kept calling, and in October 2009, I decided I wanted to attend Denise's class in May 2010. So I sent my deposit and made the commitment to go. I had to keep my word to myself in order to honor my soul.

In January 2010, I could not get time off work to go to the USA, so I rang to cancel my booking. Denise answered the phone. Since I was now talking to my mentor, my heart skipped a beat and my soul connected. I felt blessed. I then talked to Meadow, Denise's daughter, saying "I don't want a refund as I WILL be attending another time." She asked me if I was interested in coming in September 1st to 9th that year to a course that was not yet advertised. Feeling the numerology as another positive sign, I said "Yes, book me in and I *will* see you in September." Wow, such conviction! I even surprised myself at how much I had changed since April 2008. I was really grateful that I had followed my soul's guidance to get where I am and become who I was meant to be.

Having now committed to going to the USA in September 2010, I opened my heart up for the signs and guidance I needed. I have learnt that when I try to control the outcome and live in my head, it makes it so much harder for my dreams to come true. When I surrender it up to my soul and live in my heart, everything falls into place and works out 'better than I could have ever imagined'. When I hear these words, I know the soul has taken care of the details and the outcome.

I completed the Journey Practitioner course in March 2010, with huge changes in and around me on all levels. During this 18 month course, I had met a friend who was also interested in meeting Denise Linn and who said she would love to go with me. She asked if I wanted to travel around Italy with herself and her children on the way back from California. This would mean being overseas for a whole month, by far the longest I had been away from my husband and family! So the fears started to creep in again... What about the money, getting time off work, I couldn't speak Italian and didn't really know this woman I was going to travel with ... But I kept breathing in God's will and breathing out my will, trusting that everything would work out by my soul's perfection.

In the next few months, looking back on it now, it was incredible how my soul behind the scenes and beneath the surface was weaving an amazing story, and unfolding it effortlessly. It reminds me of Moses parting the Red sea, without effort. My husband started taking over my role; the kids started asking him for the advice and also taking more responsibility; work offered me a higher position for 6 weeks before I left; connections were made overseas; the travel agent offered unbelievable discounts; the timing was worked to a tee for meeting with my friend's children in Rome for the drive around Italy for eight days, and then four days by ourselves with friends of friends.

Another of Denise Linn's sayings is "beneath the surface, it's happening." Wow wasn't that the truth! I know now to just leave things out of my mind and back in my heart, and everything works out perfectly.

We arrived in California for the Soul Coaching and Past Life regression course. When I reached the Labyrinth at the top of the hill overlooking Denise Linn's property, I gave thanks to Grandfather Sun, the universe and to my soul for bringing me here to Summerhill Ranch. What a moment to remember and be grateful for! I was

> ### Manifesting Dreams
>
> *AFFIRMATION: My dreams are coming true!*
>
> *Life goes in cycles. There is a time for planting seeds and a time for harvesting bounty. Right now is your time for harvesting. Your innermost dreams and desires are manifesting. Don't stop the flow by doubting the process. All is unfolding according to your highest good.*

'living the life of my dreams' by following the guidance of my soul. In California, the sun sets into the ocean, whereas where I live in Australia, it rises over the ocean. So on the Labyrinth at Summerhill, I felt like I had reached the other end of the rainbow. I gave thanks, feeling so grateful and so blessed for my soul's journey so far, with more to come.

The ranch, teachings, friendships made, and memories taken were more than I could have imagined or even dreamt of (the soul's gift). I also learnt that I was an Indian brave in a Past Life, giving the connection to my childhood. On the day of leaving the ranch, I was sad. But inside I was so excited and proud. A new spark of my soul had awoken, again.

Italy! I couldn't sleep past 2.30am because of the jet lag, so I would sit in the bathroom and read or write until daylight. And then the days of sightseeing would begin. I felt like a little kid, in awe of everything, absolutely savoring every moment, every minute, as I didn't know if I would ever come this way again. I was like an ADHD child – here, there and everywhere at once, walking so fast, seeing as much as I could, knowing that what I saw was enough for me, not having regrets ever of what I didn't do, taking more than enough photos, but knowing that I could never reclaim that moment again, honoring the time my soul had given me, here and now. Every day I said my intention that "I allow whatever my soul needs me to hear, see, feel or know today, and I will accept it all." What a trip I had! The sights, people, experiences and memories 'were more than I could have imagined or dreamt'. I still pinch myself over all the extra bonuses, blessings and dreams that came true for me on this trip. Wow, I am truly blessed!

As a child, for as long as I can remember, I had been bullied. Then I changed myself into the people-pleaser to 'fit in', making sure others had happy memories, felt loved and heard, and were given whatever I had to give. I forgot about me and my own needs, longing for others to return the favor. Sometimes when they did, I couldn't accept it or didn't know how to, as that was how I was programmed throughout childhood. This dream trip to train with Denise Linn, and beyond, helped me to find myself, stand up for myself, allow myself my own freedom to choose what and whom I like and don't like. This was the dream trip of a lifetime for me, and I made the most of it, without regret.

Denise Linn's training has taught me that I am not my identity, the one given to me by my parents, family, friends, school, career, life etc. Who I truly am is much more magnificent, remarkable and eternal. I have learned not to judge these patterns ingrained into me, simply observing and accepting this part of me. My 'Soul Loves the Truth' and I know that by following my soul, I will achieve inner peace to be myself, not what others expect me to be.

While on this trip I became stubborn when I needed to, not wanting to be led or to follow others if I didn't want to. I wanted to make this my time and my journey, to not have regrets and resentment when I return to Australia – that I didn't do, see, or touch this or that when I was there in that space and time. I even spoke up to dominating people, though quivering inside, knowing I was fighting for my trip, my time, my money, and not accepting other people's excuses to have their choice over mine, or I would do it on my own. I wasn't afraid anymore.

The changes that happened have continued to be part of my life. Wow, how I have changed from the person I once was to who I am now! During all these changes since 2008, many people around me were separating and divorcing, some friends drifting away, with new positive, supportive friends coming into my life.

My husband was getting very concerned that we would follow the same path of separation. I told him these people had been living another identity and not being true to themselves, that I wouldn't ever stay in this marriage if I didn't love him or in any other relationship I have – I would 'never sell my soul to the devil and live a dead existence, ever again!'. My husband and children all respect and support what I learn, live, love and do; they witness and like my positive changes and also the changes in my clients. This year, 2012, after four years since the beginning of my real soul journey, beginning with reading Denise Linn's book, we are coming up to 30 years of marriage, more abundant in every way we choose, and life is unfolding through our dreams and goals, daily.

Our yacht is called *Dream n'On*. We bought her in December 2007, just before I started my soul journey. Synchronistic events brought her into our life at the time, and it felt like another 'sign' when I saw the name. My husband loves to sail her, and I love to relax and recharge my energy while on her. On every trip I thank her for being in our life. We have had so much fun and good times on her. Today we looked at a new yacht called 'Spirit Chaser'. I wonder what my soul is guiding me towards now?

Your Soul Journal

> *The understanding of who you are can never be told by another. It is only when you reach into the wellspring of your being that the truth of the soul springs forth.*

—DENISE LINN

It is a known fact that people tend to only speak about the things they think other people want to hear. We all avoid divulging the real emotional pain in our hearts. Writing in your Soul Journal connects you to that hidden emotional pain, allowing it to be energetically expressed through honesty and truth, by writing down how and what you feel.

Children tell it like it is, expressing themselves openly and honestly. For example: "I hate that food" or "I don't like that man!" Whereas adults have been programmed not to say what they mean and how they feel, repressing inwardly! When asked after a traumatic event, "Are you okay?" adults will often answer "I'm fine." Meanwhile, inside, they are being eaten up by their emotional pain.

Here is a very effective exercise which will bring you to direct soul connectedness, clearing the life matters that you cannot control, to allow you to live the Life of your Dreams.

First you will need a journal to use for your own personal Soul Journey, charting daily progress towards your dream life. Find a journal that you really like and decorate it the way you wish to, allowing your inner child to come forward and have fun! When you connect with the inner child and your soul, magic happens spontaneously in your life through synchronistic events. It's just amazing!

The first sacred ceremony we are going to perform is the Soul to Universe Contract. This contract works on the energetic field, the universe conspiring with your soul to bring into your life what your soul needs and desires in life. Just trust that even if you can't see it, it is all happening automatically. Write your sacred contract out on beautiful paper; sign it, date it and paste it at the beginning of your Soul Journal.

"I _____ (Name), do hereby declare to myself and my Creator that I will dedicate the next _____ (Months) to connecting with my soul. I will endeavor to be honest with myself and with others, to uncover the truth about who I am. Additionally, during this time, I vow to take time every day to relax and eat according to my nutritional needs rather than my emotional needs. I accept that adhering to this contract attests to the strength of my character."
Signed: _____ Dated: _____

The Soul Journal is then used to write Gratitude and Surrender entries – the more grateful we are for what we have; the more we receive from the universe. When you surrender the outcome, whatever you cannot control will come back to you 'better than you could have imagined'. You can divide the journal up with Gratitude entries on the Left side of the page, (Receiving side), and at the top line of that page write 'I am extremely grateful to the universe for:' Then on the Right side of the page, for Surrendering (Leaving side), write on the top line of the page 'I now surrender with strength to the universe."

Underneath both sentences, from the heart, write down your desires and your fears. Use dot points and leave a space in between each entry. An amazing thing happens within a couple of hours or days after you write the surrender entry; it magically turns into a gratitude entry. If you have a lot of issues around the surrendering of childhood traumas which you don't wish anyone to read, write these on a separate piece of paper with every ounce of personal honesty, but do not read it again. Then burn or shred it, allowing the universe to take over, to allow full karma and healing to occur on all levels, for all concerned. Feel the new-found freedom and inner peace fill your heart, soul and body, opening you up to new possibilities for manifesting the life of your dreams.

Flying Free

*AFFIRMATION: I unfurl my
wings and fly!*

*Be Daring. Cast aside conventions and
restrictions. Dance. Laugh. Explore.
Go beyond your predictable behavior,
and say yes to life! By doing so, you
support others in finding their wings.*

AGNES A. HOFER
Scheiblingkirchen, Austria

AGNES A. HOFER first got in touch with Soul Coaching® in the summer of 2007. Doing the Soul Coaching® program herself then, and in the years since, has had a major impact on her personal growth. So she decided to become a professional Soul Coach herself in the summer of 2010.

She holds a Master's degree in psychology from the University of Vienna (as well as further trainings in industrial/organizational and positive psychology) and a Bachelor's degree in musicology.

Besides her job as a research assistant at a business school she is training and working as a professional singer and speaker.

Agnes believes that consciousness and awareness are the keys to leading a responsible, fulfilled life. Providing the Soul Coaching® program for people who want to increase their levels of awareness is one of her contributions towards helping people to lead responsible and fulfilled lives. To contact her please visit www.soulcoaching.at

Doing Things Differently – The Road to Change

AGNES A. HOFER

Just wanting to experience more joy in one small area of your life can work miracles that extend to all other areas of your life.

*E*verything is dull. You feel stuck. You're fed up with most things that happen around you and – more importantly – *to* you. You go to school and come back home. You go to work and come back home. Wherever you're going you're always returning to the same place you started from. Your colleagues seem to lack any civilized manners. Your family drives you crazy (which actually might be pretty normal every now and then). Your life is grey, a constant struggle, sometimes more, sometimes less. But nevertheless it's 'a struggle'.

Maybe you happen to be having thoughts like: "Why do I always have to let people take advantage of me?!" "Why do I always fall for that kind of guy/girl, when I know I'm going to get hurt?!" "When will I ever get it right?!" Judging yourself can be such an exhausting undertaking...

When it comes to other people, you might also be familiar with thoughts like "Why is he/she always picking on me?" "I know that you have that great new car and yes, I know you've been to this great summer vacation. Bravo! But please stop rubbing it in." It's true: the people you have to deal with on a constant basis can be a blessing or a challenge.

And time! Yes, time... "If I had as much time as you do, *I* would accomplish at least twice as much as you have! So stop bragging about your achievements."

If some of these thoughts apply to you, you also might feel cranky when these thoughts arise. You probably don't like being that way though. I assume you'd like to get to a place where the behavior of your fellow humans doesn't have such a big impact on your emotional equilibrium. I recently heard a story about someone who wanted to ask a very busy person a brief question and got turned down quite rudely. She responded to this by saying: "I understand that an overloaded system reacts aggressively." Do you want to be the person who reacts that way? The question is: how can you get out of such an uninspiring and disempowering state of constant annoyance? What can you do *in spite of* these adverse conditions?[1]

---

1   Sometimes it is necessary to fight those conditions though, since we are not only responsible for our own lives but also to some extent for those of our fellow beings.

How can you claim your right to experience peace and joy? How can you live a meaningful life based on happiness, peace and beauty?

A tempting and quite likely thought might be: "If I could just make everyone change; if the circumstances would only change…" Well, here's the thing: you can't make everybody else change magically, but you can make *yourself* [2] *change naturally* – and this is going to have a powerful effect on you and everything and everyone else. And what's most important: You will have the feeling of being in charge again!

Okay, okay. I can hear your first reaction… "Yeah, but it isn't my fault that 'x' never learned any social manners" or "*I* am behaving flawlessly; it's *their* actions that are in need of improvement." Well, there may be some truth to this, but still the working point is not *out there*. It might be wiser to look a little closer, because: what can you *really* impact directly? And what's the one constant in your life? Hmm… Here's a little tip: it's you! And that's the good news!

Wouldn't it be great if you had that person you'd like to teach at your disposal at any time of the day, and could try new things whenever you liked? Well, it is actually that simple, when you're working with yourself!

When I was at the end of my psychology studies at the University of Vienna in 2008, I was under a lot of pressure finishing up because I wanted to do it in the minimum time (which is commonly not the rule). While finishing my diploma thesis I thought I couldn't make it to the final oral exam in such a short time. I'd had only weeks in which to prepare where others usually took months! But I wanted to do it. So I decided to take another route. Instead of worrying whether I'd make it and being a bundle of nerves, I found myself another strategy and said "Worrying doesn't help – taking action does!" Every time I started to worry again I reminded myself of this. And it worked. Despite the usual deadline panic, I consciously adopted a positive attitude and didn't join the widespread hysteria. In stepping off the common path, I changed my whole perception of the situation and had the chance to study in a focused manner and in the best possible way for my finals. It was a change that paid off.

To alter things means to initiate a change somewhere. The easiest way to do that is to start with ourselves. By doing this we also pave the way for others who want to follow this example. Like ripples in the pond, your initiative can reach much further than 'just' to your own inner thinking and behavior. When one detail of a system changes, the system will reorganize and adjust itself to the shift. It's the same for nature as it is for human beings. Thankfully (human) nature is constructed as a self-adapting entity!

---

2   *Yourself* is used here to mean your actions and reactions (towards situations and people), your thoughts and beliefs (about life, yourself and the world), your perceptions (of everyday life events), your (disempowering) habits, etc.

Additionally, once you start taking your fate into your own hands, you will (re) gain the feeling of freedom and self-determination. *You* will be your fortune's master.

Alright, we now know who we can work with most effectively – ourselves! But we might also be interested to know what we actually can 'work' with.

To release any thoughts of resentment, guilt or judgment about our own and other's behaviors, it might be useful to first know why we are doing certain things. In part, it is because we're 'modeling' (i.e. copying) them. Think of yourself when you were very little. Did your parents or the person that brought you up ever tell you that you were doing things just like they did? We often see kids behaving like their parents or other care givers. If, for instance, they use certain words, by habit their kids will start using those words too. If parents speak to each other in a disrespectful way, their children will most likely interact in the same manner with other people. On the other hand, if the parents communicate in a loving, caring way, their children are more likely to incorporate this attitude into their own behavior.

This mechanism was described scientifically a while ago by Albert Bandura who coined the term *observational learning*.[3] In his social learning theory he postulated that this particular kind of learning can occur with live models, through verbal description of a behavior or by means of media (i.e. TV). So to quite a large extent, we began learning how to behave in the world through our first encounters, with our 'significant others'. This does not mean that we start criticizing our parents' educational styles. They most probably did the best they could, as far as they knew. This in turn is just (or maybe the opposite of) what they learned when they were raised by their own parents. The important thing is to be aware of these mechanisms and to recall them every now and then, to put these experiences into the proper perspective, and to understand them and therefore feel compassion.

Every one of us does things because we saw or experienced them somewhere and they paid off. Unfortunately, a lot of behaviors today probably serve as defense mechanisms, or as methods of getting other people into defensive positions before we end up there ourselves – think of the bully in the schoolyard. The common ground for this is fear: fear of failure, fear of limitation or even fear of success. Some behaviors might have simply become habits as we repeat them over and over again. The good thing is: you can identify those habits! Doing the Soul Coaching program for instance can assist you profoundly in discovering those habits which are empowering for you, and those that are not. It also helps to ask yourself "Does this behavior really serve me?"

Broadening your awareness and gaining a clear picture of yourself is one of the most worthwhile pursuits in life. Through honest self-reflection, you get the means

---

3   Bandura, Albert, Grusec, Joan E., & Menlove, Frances, L. "Observational Learning as a function of symbolization and incentive set." *Child Development, 37,* 1966.

to propel yourself forward and truly know yourself. You stop being at somebody else's mercy (emotionally) and start acting independently, being able to lead a fulfilled and self-determined life.

He who knows others is wise.
He who knows himself is enlightened.

—LAO TZU

Speaking of acting independently, you might think of the way you usually respond to people in a conversation: are you *re-acting* to the person you're talking to or are you *acting* out of your own volition? Marie, a client of mine, realized that she tended to 'model' the way her conversational partners were talking to her. In diverging from her own point of view and her way of speaking, she was diverging from her true self to please others, thus feeling uneasy. She needed this discovery to stop disregarding her own opinions, and this empowered her substantially. She realized that she didn't need to play small and adjust to others to lead a fruitful conversation. She accepted her right to stand tall. After all, everyone has something special to contribute that's unique to that person. Let's keep that in mind and honor it.

> ### Breaking Barriers
>
> AFFIRMATION: *I am expanding beyond limitations into joy and freedom!*
>
> *There are times to go with the flow, but this isn't one of them. Now is the time to break through self-imposed barriers. Gather your inner forces, and break free from whatever is holding you back.*

A few years ago I learned about an interesting theory that's called the *Broken Windows Syndrome*.[4] Maybe you've heard about this theory too. Readers from the United States may be aware of 'public' experiments that took place in US cities from the 1980s onwards. Basically, this theory states that if you have a deserted, uncared for area (i.e. buildings with broken windows, litter on the sidewalks etc.) this area is soon likely to exhibit even more broken windows and litter on the streets. To put this in a setting of social interaction: if the conduct in a particular group starts becoming inappropriate, even more members of the group lose their inhibition to display that originally inappropriate behavior. When no one seems to care, individuals stop bothering too. I find this theory very intriguing.

---

4   Wilson, James Q., & Kelling, George L. "The Police and Neighborhood Safety." *The Atlantic Monthly*, 1982.

If this theory works one way, it might also work the opposite way too, for example, as a *Cleaned Windows Syndrome*.

Imagine your kitchen, on an average day, perhaps rather messy. Now imagine the same kitchen meticulously cleaned. Everything is neat and tidy: clean work surface, everything in its place, fresh towels ready to polish the dishes... When you prepare a meal in this normally messy kitchen, would you spill things, leaving your plate unwashed on the counter, the remains of food drying up? Or would you want to maintain this new, shiny, pretty and clean state of your kitchen?

Of course everyone's reaction will differ slightly here. But I assume that there will be a tendency towards sustaining the 'clean' status once you've experienced the shift of energy. And why shouldn't this be applicable to general standards of human behavior too? When one individual starts raising the bar, be it in terms of use of vocabulary, the way they dress, or something else, there's a chance that this will influence their surroundings. Granted, the altered behavior or attitude holds some attractiveness to the people surrounding them, and is something that's aspired to and achievable. Otherwise one might earn curious looks, whispering, or even jealous comments. It's also important that the wish for improvement or change does exist. When no one feels the need for change, and cannot see any reason to do things differently, it won't be on the top of their list. It's the same for everyone. But the fact remains, if you wish to get different results from life, you have to *do* things differently.

If you change nothing, nothing will change.

So, do *you* want to get more out of life? Do you want to break free from dis-empowering behaviors and discard self-limiting beliefs and let go of feelings of unease? Would you like to start encouraging yourself instead of judging yourself? And do you like the idea of being your life's navigator? Well, the solution is to start moving and allow yourself to experience some positive change!

If you do what you've always done,
you will get what you've always gotten.

−DENISE LINN[5]

An easy way to start manifesting change is in altering little things, like routines. Remember: If you don't change anything, nothing will change. It's in small things that big changes begin. Also there's momentum in beginnings. Once you make the decision to step up for yourself to make a difference in your life, you create a

---

5   Linn, Denise. Soul Coaching. 28 Days to Discover Your Authentic Self. Hay House, 2003.

blueprint and an energetic shift for further changes. It's just that you have to take the first step. And everything else will follow.

One of my favorite quotes says:

Take the first step in faith.
You don't have to see the whole staircase, just take the first step.

—MARTIN LUTHER KING, JR.

Often it's the overwhelming idea of getting everything done at once that keeps us from getting started in the first place. But every successful journey started with a first step. Once you're on the road, you'll gain the courage and means to go on and take the next step. You don't have to know everything at the very beginning. So start with little things, moving out of your comfort zone.

Here's one example for a feasible change of routines: Given you take the same route to work every day, why not vary the route a little? If you go by car, you can change the route in a way that allows you to see more of nature while beginning your day (watching your carbon footprint of course). This will have a soothing and harmonizing effect on your psyche as well as a de-stressing influence on your body. Studies have shown that the amount of nature and especially the amount of 'green' around us has substantial positive effects on health and overall well-being. So why not take advantage of this possibility if you can? And if you're using public transport, I suggest including the opportunity to experience more of nature too. Why not get off one stop early and walk the rest of the way, especially if there's a park nearby? I like to do this when going to certain places. When walking from the train station, I choose the way that offers an abundance of green spaces during the daytime, including both trees and grassy areas. After all, humans were designed to live with nature, not with concrete. Little changes in your routine like this can contribute to your well-being as you might experience a comfortable physical activation level, leading to a more relaxed attitude, thus leading to getting along better with your colleagues. What a perfect beginning for your new 'change-projects'!

In the 28-Day Soul Coaching Program there's a whole week dedicated to 'taking action' and one day's assignment in particular is about stepping out of your comfort zone and breaking a habit. After preparing yourself in the weeks before by practicing introspection and taking an honest look at yourself and your relationships, this is the week to step up and take action. This is actually my favorite week!

When I first did the Soul Coaching program myself in 2007 I had so much fun during that time doing everything differently. Really, almost everything. I started the day with the other foot, opened every single door with the other hand, took other routes through the house, etc. Every time I wanted to do something the way I normally did it, I thought of another (fun) way of doing it. They were tiny things, but they really got my creative juices flowing.

Denise Linn mentions an impressive study that explored cancer patients and their remission rates. The people in the group who were asked to completely change their routines, hairstyles, clothing styles, etc. were found to experience a profound shift in the way they saw themselves and their lives, and also displayed higher rates of spontaneous remissions compared to the control group. The theory was that outer change had an effect on the inner self. I found this quite intriguing. So besides shifting your perspective and deepening your awareness, this conscious breaking of habits can bring you joy and possibly contribute to your overall well-being.

Small changes like this can help you loosen your rigid routines, thus letting a fresh breeze into your life, and creating the basis for new opportunities. When you question your routines and try taking a close look at them, you might find further ways to stir things up a little. It's like looking for something you lost in a tiny pond: you might have to swirl things up with a stick 'to get a better look.' At first it's all messy and murky. After some time, sand and soil start to settle again in a new order and you can see things clearly again. Now you're able to take another look, and eventually find what you were looking for. And maybe you'll discover something else, something wonderful that you were not even looking for! Sometimes you have to stir up your life a little to cast a glance at the things that need attention, or to see 'possibilities' that were hidden from you until then. Bringing some *action* into your murky routines can work wonders. So let's do it!

You don't even have to change big things to achieve amazing results. Just wanting to experience more joy in one small area of your life can work miracles that extend to all other areas of your life. And isn't experiencing more joy in itself a sufficient motivation?

So let's shake and stir!

Change Your Habits – Change your Life

> *Life isn't about waiting for the storm to pass.*
> *It's about learning to dance in the rain!*

—ANONYMOUS

First of all, make a list of the things you do on a more or less regular basis, like preparing breakfast, riding the bus, brushing your teeth, etc. When you're spending time with something on a regular basis it can add up to quite a lot of time, even with things you do for only 5 minutes a day. This time holds great potential to be enhanced towards something you really desire. So let's play detective!

Then sort through these things by number of occurrence. The things you do or that happen most often go at the top of your list, followed by those things you do less often. It's not so much about the time you spend on each of these activities, rather it's the regularity with which you do them. As practice makes perfect, so does repeating changes to your routine. When you have a top ten 'routines list', think of ways you could juice up each of the items.

When considering what gives you joy, try to find some new ideas about how to combine a 'boring' routine with something that makes your heart sing, for instance, brushing your teeth. To enhance this routine with fun, and depending on how much time you spend on cleaning them, you could play some music while you are in your bathroom. Who says that you can't combine brushing with some movement? Alternatively, you could try doing some gymnastic exercises to contribute something positive to your physical health.

The point is, whatever time you spend doing routines that don't demand your full attention – driving the car *means* driving the car! – enhance them for whatever purpose you choose, be it experiencing more fun, joy, peace, gratitude, health or beauty in your life. You have the power to insert meaningfulness into every situation. Go get creative!

Here are some ideas on infusing your routines with new meaning and purpose:

Ways to enhance your routines with FUN and JOY

While blow drying your hair, try to move every muscle of your face at least once. And then, double speed! Find ways to have fun with your mirror image – it's a reliable partner. Besides, it's good for the blood circulation.

While waiting for the tea kettle to boil or your food to cook, try to recite a rhyme you learned in childhood (that's a challenging one!) Alternatively, try to sing your favorite TV show's theme song – in a different pitch than your normal voice.

Ways to enhance your routines with PEACE and GRATITUDE

While making your bed in the morning, take a few moments to picture yourself throughout the coming day. See yourself happy, content and interacting harmoniously with everyone you're going to meet that day.

As you're taking a shower or bath in the evening, review the previous day, and think of all the things that you can be grateful for. As Denise Linn says *"Where intention goes, energy flows"*. What you focus on expands. In paying attention to positive things, you pave the way for them to happen (again).

Ways to enhance your routines with HEALTH

This is an old one, but still very useful. Take the stairs instead of the elevator when you get the chance to. (Note: No texting walking the stairs!)

When you take out the garbage or prepare it for pick up, take 5 deep breaths *after* you've completed your task. Whenever you have to leave the house for a few moments, take the opportunity to provide your body with a good dose of fresh oxygen. When you have a little more time on your hands, take a short walk around the house or the neighborhood, concentrating on deep and full breaths.

Ways to enhance your routines with BEAUTY

Every now and then gift yourself with your favorite flowers. Just because.

These ideas are just to get you started. I'm sure you'll find a lot more ways to use your routines for your own benefit. And just in case you feel silly at some point – what the heck!? Do it anyway, whenever you feel like it. Everybody needs to find their own way of bringing joy into their days. As long as you don't do any harm to yourself or others, do whatever you need to bring more light into your days. This will not only benefit you, but also the people you're interacting with. Given the choice between choosing the Grinch or someone enjoyable as your lunch partner, you wouldn't choose the Grinch, right?

After all, our life consists of experiences and emotions. You can't have control over everything that happens to you, but you do have control over how you respond to things. Remember: "Life isn't about waiting for the storm to pass. It's about learning to dance in the rain!" When you have the chance to shape some of your experiences that lie in your sphere of action, choose the good ones. We were not meant to endure hardship by default. We were born to evolve and thrive, not only in terms of biological evolution but also in matters of the heart. When you bring more joy into your life, you will touch and light up the people around you. And as you raise your own bar, you are helping humanity to do the same.

Further Suggestions

1. *Try something new.*
   Choose one thing you always wanted to do or try, and go ahead and just do it! This will create a blueprint for more personal freedom, courage and openness.

2. *Make a list of any negative and disempowering habits you might have.*
   Try to diminish at least one of them. It might be worthwhile identifying where you experience negative situations over and over again, and developing a plan not to repeat these.

3. *Create new rituals in areas that need your attention most.*
   For instance: to focus on your blessings, create a Joy or Gratitude Journal where you write down the things you're most grateful for. This can be a great ritual for starting or closing your day.

∽

JP AMES

Westminster, Colorado, USA

On a Clear Day You Can See Forever! The title of this musical play reminds JP of the continuous unceasing flow of air that provides the means for cleansing, rejuvenating, and refreshing any space when channeled properly. In *Clearing the Way,* she realized that her living environment, as well as the space between her ears, had to be gently cleansed, revitalized, and refreshed daily in order to see clearly.

Through daily spiritual practice, JP calmly released the relentless quest to find external solutions through workshops and consultants. In silence, she became receptive to the gentle guiding whispers of her soul. This new intuitive connection opened her heart to move forward with confidence to change from the inside out.

JP accepted the challenge of freeing herself from clutter and the constant appearance of disarray and confusion by boldly taking the action steps she likens to dancing. Through every movement and orchestrated action, renewed aliveness filled the space around her, allowing the flow of her activities and thoughts to brighten and flourish, becoming illuminated like a beacon of light in the night.

Stepping forth to embrace change from the inside out, JP is now *Unstoppable* in creating a beautiful, harmonizing melody from within. She exemplifies unwavering faith in the dynamic changes that present themselves to benefit the well-being of others and herself in – *Clearing the Way* for abounding happiness and orderliness.

JP is certified in Soul Coaching® and Past Life Regression and can be reached at jpcandoit@mac.com

Clearing the Way

JP AMES

My plan is to blast out of my consciousness the 'Clutterosaurus' mentality and master my clutter with the mentality of a 'Clutter Control Manager'.

Do you feel a heightened sense of hope and expectation in the air at the beginning of each New Year? Do you look forward to those extravagant and grandiose celebrations that are planned for months and robustly engaged in across the planet, with the focus on that magical moment when the clock strikes midnight? Ten, Nine, Eight, Seven, Six, Five, Four, Three, Two, One – Happy New Year! Gala festivities around the world ring in the New Year with the singing of traditional songs, fireworks, the throwing of streamers, bells ringing, whistles blowing, corks popping, and elated exuberance shared between family, friends and neighbors.

This enchanted hour of the New Year awakens our refreshing childlike anticipation to confidently live out our planned resolutions, made with the highest motivational intentions. With every New Year, the collective universal energetic expectation for change and renewal is at its ultimate high. Within this grand flow of jubilance, we plan perfect behaviors to produce a New Year makeover, invoking the desired results. Unfortunately, these exhilarating high-spirited hopes are often dramatically followed by a rapid deflation of intentions. The expectations of *Clearing the Way* and putting into practice new behaviors for the long-sought-after life changes often fade away within days. The strategic plan animating our best intentions to make lifestyle improvements become short-circuited, causing a restriction of the energy surge meant to activate the New Year's best dreams. Has this ever happened to you?

My experiences have been humbling. For a number of New Years, including 2012, I have made impetuous resolutions relating to the issue of clutter clearing, but have (figuratively speaking) landed flat on my face. 'Ouch'! It has been painful and yet I continue to pick myself up, brush myself off, and step out to find a successful way to manage clutter.

So here I am standing grounded and balanced ready to take a gallant step toward transforming my clutter control issues and sharing my truth along the way. As I journey through the highs and lows relating to the removal of clutter from my life, my path has run into a few dead ends and unexpected curves. However, there is nothing to fear, because the universal GPS (Global Positioning System) is divinely guiding and mapping my route for *Clearing the Way*.

Even after purchasing and reading several excellent books specifically dealing with clearing clutter, space clearing, and Feng Shui, I have yet to conquer my clutter! In fact, a few years ago, I dubbed myself as a *Clutterosaurus* (a self-created word). Indeed! What prompted such a designation?

Looking as far back as my childhood, I remember living in a house that always appeared neat and tidy. Yet, to open a drawer, a closet, or dare go into the attic was like breaking the seal of an over pressurized can of soda. The outward show camouflaged the secrets that were hidden behind the neatly built-in drawers and cabinets. When leaving home to attend college and join the military, I found myself moving often without the luxury of such built-in drawers and cabinets. My frequent moves allowed the notorious *Clutterosaurus* to gain momentum. Gradually the propulsion of the *Clutterosaurus* became the shield that protected me from the world, as well as from myself. I created a built-in excuse system for anything and everything that was not accomplished or that could not be accomplished, saying that it was because of... clutter.

This has given rise to the ongoing theme of battling clutter and struggling to keep my home neat and tidy for a number of years. I noticed it more specifically after giving birth to two children and managing all of their toys and extra furniture necessary for the livelihood of the wee ones. Fortunately, through a Mother's Support Group that I co-facilitated, studying the organizational practices of two sisters who called their program 'Sidetracked Home Executives', the clutter remained manageable. Then the unexpected 'Big D' happened, and everything plummeted dramatically. After staying at home with the children since birth, who at the time of the divorce were four and eight, I was thrust into figuring out which career direction to pursue, where I was going to establish my household, and how I could provide the highest quality of care for the children. Pressing forward, I got everything working again by moving fifty miles south of Fort Collins to take up residence in Boulder, Colorado.

As the years passed, I found myself thriving on attending workshops, taking classes and working in the real estate industry. At one point, a woman who had a home business hired me for a temporary bookkeeping assignment. Excitedly, she told me all about how she was decorating her home following the principles of Feng Shui. It sounded intriguing, yet quite foreign to me. I just continued on my merry way managing my home clutter sometimes and then at other times it seemed like the clutter was managing me. Unfortunately the unmanageable appearance of clutter seemed to be the norm.

While chatting with an attendee at a seminar, the subject of clutter came up and she mentioned the book *Sacred Space*, by Denise Linn. She raved about it, detailing its Native American and Feng Shui aspects, and the different ceremonies and rituals that can be performed to dramatically change the energy in the home environment. Man I was sold! I thought to myself – Wow! This is just what I need to change things around. When this lady was kind enough to gift me the book, I was psyched and began making changes.

A few months later, I spoke with a woman who actually did home makeovers using the concepts of Feng Shui as discussed in Denise Linn's book. Fantastic! I figured my small steps could turn into big steps, so I hired her and my condo was transformed in a matter of days. It was a total rejuvenation and it felt wonderful. Unfortunately within a short period of time, the clutter started creeping back in, and the seemingly magical energy was replaced with the humdrum energy that had filled the space before the makeover. What was this about?

I had no explanation. Being clueless, I just kept following my interest and fascination with the concepts of Sacred Space and Feng Shui devouring books on the subject. My rationale was that I was just a 'learner' about these topics, thus unable to personally get the expected results. So, I did what any intelligent 'in-the-dark' seeker might do to figure out this dilemma, I maintained the vigilance of attending workshops and hiring consultants to guide me in this task of overcoming the clutter and clearing the stagnant energy issues enveloping my home. Routinely the consultants' guidance and touch created the feel of flowing energy that felt great, and I maintained the appearance of my surroundings until…

Like clockwork, after each consultation, the high would dissipate within a few weeks. I would wake up realizing that I was feeling just like I had before. Looking around, I could see that the clutter had slipped back in once again, suffocating the energy flow of my home environment. By this time, I knew that until the clutter was cleared, it was a waste of time to be concerned about 'Feng Shui' principles.

To keep the clutter under control, I had unsuspectingly fallen into the pattern of hiring consultants and receiving their suggestions. I would implement their recommendations and ideas long enough to achieve a sense of change, only to experience a setback once again. So, when I read in a brochure that a 'Clearing Clutter the Feng Shui Way' class was being offered, I signed up. The instructor mentioned that she had received her Feng Shui training through Denise Linn's Interior Alignment Design Program. On hearing this, I recalled Denise Linn's name and the book that first introduced me to her work. I absorbed the information and took extensive notes, returning home only to freeze and act as if I was attempting to perform 'brain surgery'.

Oᴋ, it was not 'brain surgery', but it might as well have been. I knew the drill: handle paper once, create a home for everything, set aside sorting and organizing time daily, keep the incoming volume of material brought into the house balanced with the disposed of or recycled stuff weekly (remembering that more needs to be thrown out or recycled in a cluttered environment), establish a designated work area, and have labeled boxes handy for sorting the papers or items needing to be handled, to prevent time wasting or getting sidetracked going to other parts of the house. In no time, the boxes were labeled, a card table set up for the work area, and sorting boxes were in place with a timer located within arm's reach. With all the steps in place, I began dividing the materials from the respective sorting boxes.

But at the end of the session, both the trash and recycle boxes held very few items. I found myself reminiscing, thinking that I might need these items someday, or wondering what if I get rid of this stuff and find out that I really do need it after all. Mind you, the majority of the boxes and things being sorted through had been in storage or taking up space in my living area for years. The inner thought dialogue was deafening and paralyzing. To eliminate the confusion and stress of the entire 'paper surgery', I walked away leaving the designated work area in place for days, weeks, or months; because I could not deal with the clutter dilemma. Each pass by the location was a reminder that I should, that I needed to do something, and yet, I was doing anything but *Clearing the Way*. It was like taking two steps forward, followed by a 100-foot back slide into the quicksand of despair. On a downward spiral, the *Clutterosaurus* designation was birthed!

Playing the role of a *Clutterosaurus* superbly, I found myself constantly being down on myself for not getting my act together, dreading the thought of having anyone over; and if the inevitable became unavoidable, the panic 'hide stuff' mode set in until the door bell rang. Talk about stress! The past has been like having an inner uneasiness nagging at me incessantly. Any hope of clearing my clutter to make way for the benefits from the Art of Feng Shui was futile! At this juncture of the challenge, I threw in the towel and gave up on mastering my clutter for an extended period of time, all the while continuing to feel an annoyance about the clutter that would not go away. It was as if from deep within my core, gentle nudges from my soul and spirit guides kept the matter of clearing clutter in my conscious mind.

During the time of smugly ignoring and denying the matter, the ability to find important papers and things that I was once able to locate in spite of the clutter began to diminish. The organization that saved me became entwined with the unmanageable disarray of clutter. One day as I was foraging through a room, I recalled a children's story about denial entitled: *There's No Such Thing as a Dragon*, by Jack Kent. The child tells his parents that there is a dragon in his room and the parents say over and over again that "There's no such thing as a dragon" until the dragon grows so large that it lifts the house right off its foundation. With a change of heart, the parents acknowledge that the child was indeed seeing a dragon. As the family recognized and loved the dragon, it grew smaller and smaller and eventually became the family pet. They all lived happily ever after with the small pet dragon fitting into the household perfectly.

By my ignoring and denying its intrusive nature, the reign of the *Clutterosaurus* became more and more powerful. Now that I had thrown in the towel and given up on conquering my chaos, the disorganization and encroaching clutter that surrounded me daily was unfavorably affecting every aspect of my life. It has been outrageously humbling to admit that I had empowered paper and miscellaneous small items (figuratively speaking) to control my life!

Therefore in November of 2011, I stopped ignoring the gentle nudges from within to clear clutter and hired a clutter consultant to work with me for three hours. Two or three boxes in the office were sorted. I placed the array of papers and items needing to be taken care of in the appropriate boxes – 'To Do' – 'Shred' – 'Throw Away' – 'Recycle' – 'Give Away' – and last but not least 'Find a Place For'. I am still working on that one! It was helpful, and yet... the room still remained less than in order and I felt daunted by having to deal with taking care of the papers and items placed in the boxes after she left. What was this all about?

This 'fresh start' was by now sounding pretty familiar and futile. It was time to seek and find an effective way to set in motion a sure-fire system to manage the clutter that surrounded me. In the book, *The Soul Loves the Truth*, by Denise Linn, she says: "I know that almost nothing is impossible if someone really believes in it." I really wanted to believe in my heart of hearts that I could take control of clearing the clutter surrounding me and establish order from the inside out. I really wanted to believe that I could dissolve my *Clutterosaurus* title and redefine myself as a *Clutter Control Manager*. That has a good ring to it – Yes! Wait a minute – "really *wanted* to believe". Denise ends her sentence by saying "... if someone *really believes* in it". Aha! The truth is that I could not vanquish the *Clutterosaurus* dilemma until I stopped sitting on the "want" fence. I had to *really believe*, not *want to* believe.

> ### Renewing Your Life
>
> AFFIRMATION: *Radiant vitality is filling my life!*
>
> *A powerful inner and outer renewal is occurring in your life. Purification is happening on many levels. Take your life to the next level by clutter-clearing. Release situations and people that don't empower you, space-clear your environment, and eat lightly. In order for renewal to occur, the old needs to make way for the new.*

Oh my goodness! Past attempts to clear the clutter and to implement Feng Shui principles had been unsuccessful because the focus had been on "wanting". I had been sitting on the "want" fence wishing and desiring for change to magically happen. While waiting for the magic, I plunged into a delusional fear-based paralysis, plagued by the unrealistic ideas that the clutter and disorganization were not that bad. In fact, the circumstances were shielding or protecting me from the world, as well as from myself. Yet because of the annoying nudges to clear the clutter, I continued to seek solutions *outside* of myself.

By hiring consultants, I expected their power and expertise to solve my dilemma and carry me through to personal order and organization. Even though this never happened, I naively rode their electrifying energy surge until it was used up. Becoming disappointed that the change did not last, it never dawned on me that my inner circuitry, or lack of its flow, could be involved in the lasting outcome. Since I was devouring the concepts intellectually, it seemed logical to me that the inner shifts were happening in spite of the way I was actually thinking. Wrong! The journey between my head and my heart was being short-circuited by the debilitating thought-choices made. Blindsided by this self-devastating path, I dismissed the subtle intuitive spiritual messages received as insignificant. Is it any wonder that the clutter concerns had escalated, instead of getting better or becoming manageable?

No! Yet, the evidence clearly revealed that I needed to take responsibility for clearing my own clutter; and that I needed to unblock my inner energetic circuitry. To accomplish this, I recognized the need to shift my perception from the outer appearances to the inner well-being of my psyche and body. By jumping down from the 'want' fence, the binding shackles of fear and disbelief could confidently be shed to begin mastering the clutter from the inside out. This grounding leap positioned me to move forward with an energetic momentum, creating the 'Unstoppable' foundation for transforming my clutter. This change was propelled by the acceptance that the real house that I dwell in is my body; and by clearing old stagnant thoughts to allow a smooth energetic flow from within.

Do you see what I see? The clutter has been the dense constricting cover-up for the internal battle to reclaim my soul power and to awaken the flow of energy throughout my body. To get right with my body, I began to exercise more, learning new energetic postures through the Art of Tai Chi Chih. Also, I took action to re-establish my creditability with my soul by acknowledging the dismissed intuitive messages. I now pay close attention to those intuitive nudges that have literally been softly saying, "Clear your Clutter" for years. Yes, I said years. More recently, the intuitive phrase has become a little longer: "Clear your Clutter, reclaim your power, and you will know what to do next." I feel that the word 'power' has been emphasized to acknowledge my soul, reminding me that I have the resources and intuitive energetic flow to take the necessary action to create an uplifting vision of my future. The spiritual guidance has been consistently present, lingering politely, softly bringing to mind ideas for change, or for the need to get organized. I give thanks that this unconditional loving presence has unyielding patience, waiting for my courage, strength, and awakening to surface, in order to birth new and empowering choices.

Two choices have significantly empowered my life. The first choice I made was in early 2009. I enrolled to attend the Soul Coaching Seminar offered by Denise Linn at Summerhill Ranch in Paso Robles, California. If I had not been introduced to her expertise through her book *Sacred Space* – creating sacred space through Space Clearing and Feng Shui – it is very unlikely that I would have pursued enrollment in her Soul Coaching certification program. Denise Linn's presence in my life has been like a twinkling star, appearing at those moments when her gracious wisdom was most needed to enlighten and spur me on. For this tender touch, I am grateful!

The second choice was to delve into *Clearing the Way* – releasing the clutter issues from the inside out to move beyond the year 2012 with a refreshing outlook on fulfilling my life's dreams. This choice has given me a deeper insight into the significant role that the flow of energy has in the environment, as well as within my body. The truth is – I have been saying that I want to change from the inside out and yet; the main focus has been on the outside. Therefore, I am consciously centering on ways that I can enliven my body from within by acknowledging it as sacred space, committing to a daily spiritual practice, studying the seven charka centers of the body, enjoying a sunset or sunrise, spending time in nature, and reading books that nurture my soul. These activities and practices have energized my soul, creating a more relaxed flowing 'interior design' of expression coming forth from my inner being. It has become very clear that it is all about the choices I make on this journey of life, choices which broaden my horizon for *Clearing the Way* to exemplify orderliness. During this year of choosing to boldly step forward, I believe that I am giving rise to the empowerment of freedom and change.

It is all about staying consciously aware that the real house we inhabit is the body, and that the daily clearing of clutter between the ears is the most important step we can take to insure that our surroundings are clutter free.

If you are someone who has had an ongoing issue with clutter in your life, can you now feel a heightened sense of hope and expectation in the air? Will you join me in taking the beginning steps of turning within to rediscover the power and strength to overcome the insidious clutter, once and for all? Are you looking forward to taking high-energy action steps to truly move forward, creating moment-by-moment successful clutter-clearing accomplishments?

The *Clutter Control Manager* is birthed as I choose to walk in the light with unwavering faith, changing my attitudes, thoughts, and beliefs with unceasing hope, courage and love. As I have only just begun this journey of managing clutter from the inside out, I truly believe in my heart of hearts that I am reclaiming my soul power and redefining myself. I am ready to be *Unstoppable* in embodying my freedom and incorporating change – *Clearing the Way* for living the life of my dreams. I am becoming stronger than my *Clutterosaurus* history on a daily basis, as I stay centered and committed to following the three-step action plan below, while consciously maintaining a clutter-free environment from the inside out.

Action Plan to Manage Clutter

This action plan is made up of three steps to electrify freedom and change, *Clearing the Way* to be a *Clutter Control Manager*.

Action Step One: Daily Spiritual Practice
The intention of this step is to open one's heart, mind, and soul to the Divine on a daily basis. The most important feature of this step is to spend time daily connecting with the Divine – no matter what!

I have established a pattern of spending a minimum of 15 minutes each morning and evening to be still with my Higher Power. If my mind chatter seems uncontrollable, in the morning I hum – "AH"; and in the evening I hum – "OM."

Action Step Two: Daily Inner Practice
The intention in this step is two-fold. First, it is to be sincerely honest with yourself about the attitudes, thoughts and beliefs that orchestrate your life. Second, it is about learning more about your body and soul through any media that works best for you. For Example: reading, journaling, dancing, and/or movement.

I am currently working on clearing the clutter between my ears. Since movement is a key mind-clearing and centering activity for me, I walk between two and five miles daily. When walking outside, I open my senses to take in all of the sights, sounds, and fragrances. Inside, I move my body in rhythm with the music I play. I acknowledge and respect my body as the real house of energy that I dwell in. I am realizing that in order to make deep changes in my life, I must clear old thoughts to get the energy flowing smoothly within. Intellectually, I am devouring the words of wisdom in *Feng Shui for the Soul,* by Denise Linn; *Feng Shui for the Body,* by Daniel Santos; and *Sacred Contracts,* by Caroline Myss.

Action Step Three: Daily Outer Practice
The intention here is to take physical action to sort, organize, and beautify the living environment around you.

I am currently spending a minimum of 15 minutes each day sorting, organizing, and refreshing my home. I am recycling and letting go of papers and things with ease. I feel that the key to Action Step Three is being steadfast in respectfully doing Action Steps One and Two. Step Three is the outward sign that the first two steps are being accomplished, to insure that a continuous alignment is being made to grow and enrich the attitudes, thoughts, and beliefs housed within my very being. Three resources that I am reading for tips on this step are: *Sacred Space,* by Denise Linn; *The Ultimate Guide to Clearing Your Clutter,* by Mary Lambert; and *Organize for a Fresh Start,* by Susan Fay West.

I initially started the plan outlined above by daily practicing the first two steps. Then I decided to gradually phase into step three because I felt that if I really stayed committed to the first two steps, step three would fall into place systematically. That is in fact what happened. I am faithfully staying committed to the daily morning and evening practices. The first sign of hope for step three came when I cleaned and rearranged my meditation room. Shortly after the clearing, I comfortably began sorting for 15 minutes, ending the session an hour later feeling great and thoroughly energized from the clearing and organization. A shift has occurred from deep within. I am now letting go of clutter easily and confidently!

The overall intention of implementing these Action Steps is to practice self-discipline, to make changes from the inside out, and to complete a 40-day plan. The goal of my plan is to blast out of my consciousness the *Clutterosaurus* mentality and master the waves of clutter with the mentality of a *Clutter Control Manager*.

I now energetically acknowledge that my body is the real house that I reside in, and that clearing the clutter between my ears is the most important step to electrify my ability to live life more fully and joyfully. Thus, I believe that *Clearing the Way* from the inside out, partnering on the journey with my Spirit Guides, is my ticket to being *Unstoppable* beyond the year 2012, and living the life of my dreams!

∽

BRIDGET P. DRIGGERS
Georgia, USA

BRIDGET HOLDS THE vision that everyone can live a life of higher purpose and achieve success while maintaining peace through balance.

Bridget Prewitt Driggers began her incredible journey at Queen Kapiolani Hospital Oahu, Hawaii. Her father's work moved them to six more states before she graduated from high school. Bridget met her husband Dave at Auburn University where she earned a B.A. in Interior Design. They settled in the N. Georgia mountains to raise their daughter and son.

Being clairsentient from early childhood, Bridget interacts with the energies of a space. She has studied feng shui with many Masters including Denise Linn. As a member of the Board for the International Feng Shui Guild, she participated in several conferences. Bridget is an intentional designer and works mostly with corporate clients who seek a worker friendly environment that also meets governmental green standards.

Gathering many tools of healing, such as space clearing, Reiki, and qigong, Bridget continued her studies with a South American shaman and became an Angel Therapy Practitioner® and Certified Spiritual Counselor through Doreen Virtue. She became ordained and is now a co-minister for a nondenominational church. With her children, she started a non-profit organization to support young adults affiliated with the Child Spirit Institute.

Through the Soul Coaching® program, Bridget helps you take hold of the highest dream that you can and use your power to attain it. She believes that nothing can stop you once your vision is clear. Contact her through www.bridgetdriggers.com

Balance Equals Happiness

BRIDGET DRIGGERS

The statement 'balance equals happiness' may sound like a cliché,
but for me it is the essence of my days.

*A*ll of my life I've had a desire to know how the world works and my place in the grand plan. It has always been my passion to study different cultures and the practices they use to make sense of the world we all live in. This desire has led me to study many forms of healing and acquire many tools which have enriched my life. This knowledge has helped me to self-evaluate and grow as a person and as an interior designer, soul coach and minister.

Reflect over the past year, and give thanks
Often we must learn the same lessons over and over. In the year 2010, I was given the opportunity to learn more about the need for having balance in my life by having a very out of balance year. Because of the economic downturn, I had very little work. But there were lots of shifts and changes going on in my immediate family as well. Our daughter-in-law delivered our grandson Joshua on March 28. Ten days later our son, Joshua's father, had major hip surgery and four days after our only daughter moved across the country from Georgia to Oregon. My daughter-in-law went back to work after her maternity leave. I supported our son, Jonathan, as he parented Joshua and worked through his own healing process, since he could not drive or do any lifting, including 9 ½ lb. baby Joshua.

When my mother had double knee replacement surgery in August that year, I traveled to be with my Dad and get their house ready for her return home after rehabilitation. Then, when my husband and I took our first vacation of the year over Labor Day weekend, he contracted a lung disease that led to a three-month illness of major discomfort. He was not able to do any lifting, yard work or house work. Family came from all around at the end of October for Joshua's christening and by December 15th, I could not move my right arm even an inch from my body in any direction. I had what they medically call a 'frozen shoulder.' Anyone could see that this was a cosmic way of telling me that I was not taking care of myself and therefore my life was extremely out of balance.

I was keeping up with my environment and I was taking care of my primary relationships, but pretty much everything else: my health, my spiritual life and both my interior design and soul coaching businesses were neglected. I was purely out of balance and my body was reminding me of that fact. The pain prompted me to immediately place my self-care and spiritual life back on the top of my priority list, but this left my environment and relationships in the background, causing me to still be out of balance. This made me very angry. Between the week of Christmas and New Year's I threw a temper tantrum followed by a pity party which then concluded in a laughing, headshaking moment of realization of the part I'd played in my own dis-comfort and dis-ease. With my right arm pretty much useless, I started the year 2011 paying better attention to my past experiences with balance. I began by revising my established plans with the renewed goal of having a better year in all ways. In the dictionary the word 'balance' means a state of equilibrium or equipoise, mental steadiness, or emotional stability; habit of calm behavior, judgment, etc. The dictionary defines happiness as being in a state of harmony. For me, balance equals happiness.

Re-examine your values and your needs
Every year, during the week between Christmas and New Year's Eve, I spend time reflecting upon the past year, giving thanks, and then setting plans for the coming year. But following the difficult year I'd just had in 2010, I did a much more in-depth evaluation of my life. It seemed like the perfect time since I had just become a grandmother, and 2011 would be my first full year of having the 'grandparent experience'. I examined my values and investigated what my primary needs were. I also spent a lot of time looking at my primary relationships, and as the year progressed, I started looking at all of my other relationships as well. I really wanted to see if the person who I thought I was, the person that I felt I communicated outwardly in the world, was the same person that my grandson sees and feels. I wanted to speculate on what his toddler brain thought my values were and discover whether they matched up in any way with what I believe are my true values.

As my investigation progressed, the one big thing that stood out for me was my need for *balance*. I have done a lot of work in the past trying to have a balanced, evenly organized and distributed life, but for some reason that year it seemed even more important. I had been given a lot of opportunities during the previous year to experience what I perceived as the opposing forces of balance and imbalance. So I spent time developing some tools that would help me to achieve the balance that I really want in my life. Being a visual learner with a degree in interior design, I work better with some form of visual representation or reminder about my intentions and how I want to spend my time.

Now that I'm in my fifties, I'm a lot more aware of how balance affects me in all aspects of my life, but especially at my core. I have also learned how very powerful 'intention work' is. What I've learned is that balance is a feeling inside of us. It shows up in the way that we speak, the very timbre of our voice. It is apparent in our breathing, our sleeping, the way we hold our bodies when we're walking or while we're sitting at our desks. Being in balance allows us to be present, truly and fully, and allows us to be the person that we want to present to the world.

Set your intentions

I've had an intention and prayer practice for as long as I can remember. My life or the resulting outcome of my intention and prayer life, sometimes looks the way I imagined it to be, but sometimes it does not resemble in the slightest the results I had pictured in my head. Yet I have found that the journey between my intention and the outcome is the most important part, because this is where all of our living takes place. Also, I know that the amount of joy we experience is directly related to the level of balance we feel and obtain in our lives. I know that the statement 'balance equals happiness' may sound like a cliché, but for me it is the essence of my days. It is the form of measurement that I have identified within myself that allows me to have a well-rounded and fulfilling life.

Make a Vision Board

At least once a year I make a vision board, and there have been times when I've also made up pie charts that represent my priorities. In the past, I have used a large planning calendar to insert different colors as a representation of all the different aspects of my life, highlighting those areas that were important to me and what I wanted to spend my time on each day. I've done all kinds of things to help myself stay balanced.

Ensure your environment supports your intentions:
Clear clutter and balance energy
Being an intentional interior designer, I regularly apply feng shui principles to my living and work spaces, using the tools that Denise Linn taught me as an Interior Alignment practitioner. I fill out my own client questionnaire with my husband, and we go around the house making adjustments to our environment so that it nurtures us. We do this by placing the bagua, or eight-sided Chinese energy template, over the floor plan of our home as well as each room in our home. Using the intentions we have noted on our questionnaire, we may move furniture, artwork, lighting, accessories or plants to achieve the proper energy flow and visual stimulus to assist us in realizing those very intentions. We perform this whenever we are feeling out of balance, when new opportunities are presented, or when doors are closed. This practice has always been very successful for me and now it is just a natural part of my life.

As an example, several years back my husband Dave, who is a chemical engineer, had taken a new job eighteen months prior. He came home on a Friday and I could tell that he was troubled, so I asked him what was going on. I did not want his mood to ruin our weekend so I said let's sit down and talk about it now. He told me how he was being scattered around through several divisions of the corporation and taking care of all kinds of tasks, but he wasn't sure if he was making a difference, whether he was contributing enough.

After a while, he shifted his thoughts and started thinking about what he did want. It boiled down to the fact that he wanted to be appreciated; he wanted to feel an integral part of the corporation at large. Two weeks prior to this conversation I had purchased a strand of nickel-sized tumbled citrine stones which give off the energy of abundance. So I went and found them, cut the strand and put them in my husband's hands. I said, "Why don't you go into every room in our home, stand at the entrance, find the career and life's journeys area, and then place one of these stones of abundance in the helpful people area of the room as it relates to the bagua template. Doing this will activate your intention of wanting to be supportive in your job and being supported in return." He placed them over door frames, under a chair cushion, and in a few vessels such as a basket, a drawer and a plant.

> ## Planting Seeds
>
> AFFIRMATION: *Seeds of grace are being planted in the fertile soil of my soul.*
>
> *The fertile soil of your soul is ready to receive the seeds that will come to harvest in the years ahead.*
> *Get clear on what you desire for yourself and your future. Timing is vital, and now is your moment to plant spiritual seeds.*

As we went on with our weekend, Dave was feeling a lot more in command of his life and pleased that he took a step to set and support his intentions. Two weeks later to the day, we were at his company Christmas party. Dave's boss unexpectedly stood up in front of everyone and told them that he had surveyed all of the employees and that they had all agreed that my husband was the most valuable employee for the year. He said that my husband was always ready to help anyone in any of the corporations divisions, and that he had contributed greatly to the growth of their business that year. He then presented my husband with a new Rolex watch. That watch now sits on my husband's wrist as a reminder to him of the power of our intentions.

Make a list of time-use categories

I'd like to share with you another set of tools that I use to achieve balance in life, and therefore happiness. In order to qualify and quantify balance, I have divided up how I spend my time into six unique areas. At any given moment I am doing something that falls into one of these categories, or several categories at the same time.

The first category is entitled *My Environment*, which entails my housekeeping, my gardening, bill paying, shopping, etc.

The second one is *Health*. This could be exercising, walking the dogs, or cooking a healthy meal from our garden.

The third category, *Relationships*, consists of my interaction with my husband of thirty-three years, my children, my sister, my parents, other family members and my friends.

The fourth category is *Spiritual Life*; this consists of my own personal prayer and meditation practice.

The fifth and sixth categories are both work related. I am an interior designer by degree so I have my *Intentional Design* business for my fifth category, which includes clutter clearing and home-staging.

The sixth is *Soul Coaching* which includes classes, seminars, group and one on one coaching, and angel communication sessions.

So I encourage you to make a broad list of your different but important time-use categories. Possibly five, six or as many as you need. Unlike the nine areas of the bagua, which do relate to all aspects of my life, the six categories that I'm speaking of are time and action related. It is how I spend the minutes of my days. How do you spend yours?

Evaluate everything you do to ensure your activities fit into your categories: Modify your list if necessary
Of course I would love to have balance in every single moment and when I do have a perfectly balanced day I am most thankful. Because I really like to see progress, I have given myself a break and decided to focus more on having a balanced week – a much more achievable goal. This also makes it much easier to see short-term positive results, which accumulate over the long term.

Basically, imbalance makes me unhappy. Maybe one week I will have done nothing but work for sixteen hours straight for seven days in a row. This makes me grumpy. I get anxious, and I am not my authentic self. This is also true if I spend too much time caregiving or being too introspective. I find that too much of anything is really not good for me.

I don't even do well after ten days at a spiritual or meditation retreat. I need contrast. I need to see the yin and yang of things in order to be inspired to continue a task. For instance at a retreat, I need the opportunity to call home and speak to my family and friends. By refocusing my attention, it allows my brain to disengage just long enough for me to go back to the task or the problem that I'm solving, becoming able to see things in a different light. Similarly, taking quick breaks to balance myself during the day allows me to appreciate my journey; it allows me to step back and get a better perspective, a broader view of what I'm doing.

Put a time value in hours per week on your activity items i.e. Your work, play, exercise, meditation time etc.
Most of us spend a large portion of our time at our job and fill in the rest of our

life around this large time commitment. We work at a single location for eight, ten, even twelve hours a day. But a growing number of people are making their livelihood at home using mobile phones and computer networks to stay connected. For the majority of my career I've worked for myself. If this applies to you, you'll know that this is a whole different kind of juggling act. If you work at home, you may sit down at your office and still work those eight hours as if you were at a corporate office. But most likely you are also weaving other areas of your life in and out of your days. This is where we can find joy and balance in small increments through the flexibility we are offered by working at home. Decide how much time you want to spend on each of these tasks, and what percentage of your week you wish to devote to each of those categories. And yes, week by week it does change, and that is when having a balanced month comes into play.

Mark out time blocks on your calendar (whether on paper, computer or phone)
You can do this yourself by starting with the 'knowns' such as the appointments we all put on our weekly calendars. Then, fill in the remaining spaces with the other categories of activities that you value. I will say that the six different areas that I have chosen as my personal categories do not all have the same value. Definitely my relationships and my spiritual practice are very important to me, but they are certainly not something that in every week I can spend the most amount of time on.

Visualize
My time management model resembles the 'rocks in a bowl' experiment. Visualize that your week is a clear container. First place into this container the larger rocks, the most important blocks of time on your calendar such as work (40 hrs.). Then add other time categories as the smaller rocks, such as exercise (6 hrs.). Keep going, all the way down to sand particles like prayer and meditation (4 hrs.) The water you pour in, surrounding all of the contents in your container, which is your life, should represent the JOY that you feel during all of your activities.

Set a time each week to plan your week ahead
I start planning my weeks on Sunday. My husband and I talk about our work and personal appointments for that week. Then I call my parents and he calls his mother and we see what's going on with them for the week. I may check in with business associates or clients by e-mail and schedule any time commitments I need to make with them. This gives me a good picture of when I will be in town working, out of town working, or working from my home office. Then I place my personal appointments on the calendar and jot down errands and items that I need to take care of personally. Then I schedule in some fun time with my husband, my family and my friends. I have a regular spiritual practice that I do the first thing every morning. Taking care of my health is woven into each day through yoga, exercise, walking etc. I am also very conscious of what I eat and drink. All

of these actions fit under the various categories that I value, and I can see my balanced week starting to take shape.

Prioritize Daily

So how do you prioritize when everything is important? You go over your weekly plan daily and adjust according to the daily priorities. Work deadlines, due bills, or appointments can be time-sensitive and take priority at times. A sick child for instance can trump any appointment or deadline. You are always in charge of your choices. It may not always feel like it but you are.

I look at my calendar and tomorrow's to-do list at the end of my day. I check off the progress I've made and prioritize actions for the next day. I may send out a few emails or make a few calls to firm up appointments. But I finish my day having a good idea of what my tomorrow will look like. And if your plans get side tracked, remember to…

Be flexible

Just as in everyone else's life, things arise. A 'fire' may need to be put out, but I adjust my schedule in my mind and diligently try to put everything back into my schedule to some degree. But if my time management completely goes off the rails, I will always go within, take a few breaths and then turn myself over to the task at hand. As they say, tomorrow is another day.

Know your roles and your goals

My week is full of many tasks. Some of them relate to my personal roles and business responsibilities and some of them are more goal or dream related. Knowing which category you place your activities in will help you set your intentions for your week and your life. Take some time to evaluate your activities, either as a whole and weekly. Make sure that you have a sufficient amount of roles, which are the same as responsibilities, and goals, which relate to your aspirations.

I think any major breakthrough in finding balance in your life depends on finding your own personal comfort zone as it relates to a timeline. By this I mean: you need to experiment with different spaces of time to find your own time-needs for balance. Do you need more or less time for specific activities than you presently have allotted? Try varying the time spaces for those categories until you find what works best for you in achieving a balanced life.

Set boundaries

I have what I refer to as firm and flexible boundaries. I am sure you do too, even if you do not know it. They can be a part of your journey as you fulfill your roles and go after your goals. One firm boundary that relates to my time is that I do not give consultations during social events or outings. I have flexible boundaries about working on weekends. If my husband needs to work on the weekend, then

I will usually set up a time for me to work also. I find that my boundaries are very firm when they relate to my values, but my boundaries can be quite flexible when it comes to spending time with my grandson! Our inner tuning forks can be a great guide when it comes to setting or bending a boundary. Listen to yourself.

Forgiveness and letting go
The times that we need to forgive ourselves usually start with our own guilt. This may come because we said "no" to someone. Sure, we want to be of service, but not to the detriment of our priorities, deadlines, or the crossing of our boundaries. Forgive yourself for feeling that you are not enough and review the previous steps.

Live and grow in joy
It is when you take the time to bring yourself into the warm embrace of balance that you do not feel resentful about what you are doing, when you are doing it, and who you are doing it for. You know that everything is a part of the wonderful life that you've created for yourself.

Bless each precious day that you have. Be proud of the fire that burns inside of you that urges you to seek your truth. My favorite modern poet, John O'Donohue says it beautifully in this poem from his book *To Bless the Space Between Us – A Book of Blessings:*

For Longing

Blessed be the longing that brought you here
And quickens your soul with wonder.
May you have the courage to listen to the voice of desire
That disturbs you when you have settled for something safe.
May you have the wisdom to enter generously into your own unease
To discover the new direction your longing wants you to take.
May the forms of your belonging – in love, creativity, and friendship –
Be equal to the grandeur and the call of your soul.
May the one you long for long for you.
May your dreams gradually reveal the destination of your desire.
May a secret Providence guide your thought and nurture your feeling.
May your mind inhabit your life with the sureness with which your body
inhabits the world.
May your heart never be haunted by ghost-structures of old damage.
May you come to accept your longing as divine urgency.
May you know the urgency with which God longs for you.

Checklist for Balance and Success

1. Reflect and Give Thanks
2. Re-examine your Values and Needs
3. Set Your Intentions
4. Make a Vision Board
5. Check that Your Environment Supports Your Intentions
6. Make a List of Time-Action Categories
7. Evaluate: See if Items Fit and Modify if Needed
8. Give Time-Action Items Value in Hrs./Week
9. Mark out Time Blocks on Calendar
10. Visualize
11. Set Aside Planning Time Each Week
12. Prioritize Daily
13. Be Flexible
14. Know Your Roles and Goals
15. Set Firm and Flexible Boundaries
16. Forgiveness and Letting Go
17. Live and Grow in Joy

∽

MARGARET PERRY
Cheshire, UK

MARGARET IS AN empathic natural guide, mentor and Soul Coach with a generous spirit. Her passion is to inspire and assist others to find fulfillment and live life more joyfully. Becoming a Certified Soul Coach and Past Life Coach helped Margaret discover her spiritual self and develop her intuitive inner wisdom.

An experienced business woman and counselor, she provides sacred space so that her clients can connect with their natural resources and discover their true pathway. Margaret holds professional qualifications in Counseling and Hypnotherapy. She is a Reiki Master Practitioner and Spiritual Healer. Contact her via www.margaretperry.co.uk

RACHEL PERRY
London, UK

RACHEL IS NATURALLY intuitive with a lively, enquiring mind. She has a genuine interest in people and is fascinated by how we're all shaped by our beliefs and values.

The prospect of surgery following a sports injury motivated Rachel to explore how the power of the mind can heal the body. This inspired her to become a Soul Coach where she discovered her gift for helping others access their innate wisdom. Rachel has a Masters Degree in Chemistry and also loves the challenge and variety of working in the corporate world. Contact her via rachel@rachelkperry.co.uk

∽

The Soul's Truth – a Mother's Perspective

MARGARET PERRY

Within each of us is a beauty and spirit so potent that with the smallest of acts,
we each have the potential to make a difference in the world.

From the moment I felt her soft, peachy skin as I gently stroked her cheek, I was truly in love with my new daughter, Rachel. It was my dream come true to realize that we were both safe. Having spent the last four weeks of my pregnancy in hospital with eclampsia, facing the reality of a breech baby, the emergency caesarian was a welcome relief.

In Victorian Britain, displays of emotion were considered a sign of weakness. Thankfully nowadays, it is commonly recognized that allowing ourselves to experience our feelings (as opposed to burying them) is a sign of inner strength. Two important lessons I have learnt through Soul Coaching are that it takes great courage to show vulnerability, and the importance of the power of thought in manifesting our dreams.

> *Each thought has the power to make our dreams come true.*
> *Swan finds her true beauty and power by listening within.*

—TREE OF LIFE INSPIRATIONS©

This powerful quote inspires me to believe that – like the intuitive wisdom of the swan – within each of us is a beauty and spirit so potent that with the smallest of acts, we each have the potential to make a difference in the world. I see this in my daughter. I love the way she has blossomed into a wise young woman who is beautiful, both inside and out.

It also reminds me of the amazing power of thought, its relationship to our personal belief system and the significant role it can play in creating the life of our dreams. It's so easy to get into the frame of mind where we feel limited by what we believe is possible. However, when we trust in the power of our dreams, we have endless possibilities.

My journey of self-discovery began when I studied Transactional Analysis (TA) in my late 20s and 30s, and then studied to become a counselor. It felt so right; it was exactly where I needed to be. I can still picture my daughter's face laughing with me as I jumped for joy when I qualified! Working as a counselor opened many new doors for me, and I thoroughly relished the challenge for several years until I found myself at a crossroads. Hindsight tells me that some of my best work has occurred during periods like this. At the time it felt as though I was dormant or stuck, yet I was merely re-grouping and quietly assessing.

To me this is akin to the way plants and flowers seem dormant throughout the winter. Spring arrives and majestic shoots burst forth, filled with strength and vitality. Unseen to the naked eye, nature has been busily working her magic beneath the ground. The fresh, young leaves are a sign of new growth, a signal of hope and vibrant possibility.

New pathways

Around this time my dear friend Liz, from whom I'd learnt the art of meditation, introduced me to Soul Coaching. The beauty of Soul Coaching is that it is a gentle program, a way forward that lets you access a window to your soul and authentic self. No matter what you tell others or what image you portray, if you are not honest with yourself you can feel diminished. However, when you truly acknowledge and accept your innermost feelings, you honor your soul. Remember, *the soul loves the truth.*

Emerging into Grace

AFFIRMATION: I open my soul to grace.

All is well. You can relax and let go, for your path is divinely guided. Gifts from the Creator are pouring into your life. Gratitude abounds. A spirit of grace is softly unfolding in your life.

Together with learning new tools to help others, I found the culture and ethos of Soul Coaching enthralling. I was captivated by Denise Linn's honest and authentic style of teaching, and especially loved the new pathways that opened inside me as a result of her insightful Soul Journeys.

I'll never forget the first time Denise guided our group through a Past Life meditation. We journeyed back through our own life to the point of our conception, then back through the lives of our ancestors too. It was a powerful, healing experience that enabled me to connect with inner wisdom, humility, creativity, and find forgiveness and acceptance. I was reminded just how important it is for me to feel connected to my family and friends, and how my values are an integral part of my identity. One of our strongest motivating forces is the need to be consistent with our identity as we perceive it.

My experience reminded me of the story of *The Ugly Duckling* in Hans Christian Anderson's fairy tale: A swan's egg rolled into a duck's nest where it hatched. The young swan's strange appearance caused the brood of ducklings to reject him. Feeling like an outcast with his stubby brown feathers, he left to search for a new home. But he was mocked and ridiculed wherever he went. After a harsh winter living by a lake, he approached a flock of migrating wild swans and was surprised when they welcomed him. He felt puzzled until he caught sight of his reflection in the water and realized he'd grown from an ugly duckling into a strong and beautiful white swan. When the flock took flight, the young swan spread his magnificent wings and flew alongside his new family. He embraced his newfound strength and identity.

Soul Coaching is the inspiration that invigorates me to live a life that is consistent with my true inner values. Like the young swan, I discovered a sense of alignment because I was in the right place for my inner self, my soul.

Clearing the way to a consistent identity

One of the wonders of Soul Coaching is exploring our connection with the elements during the 28 day program. The program dedicates a week to each of the elements: Air, Water, Fire and Earth. Each week focuses on clearing a different aspect of your life. Have you ever noticed how something magical happens whenever you clear out a drawer, a space, a thought, or something to which you have a strong emotional tie? I usually find that something new (and often better) quickly fills the space I have created.

Air week focuses on mental clearing and connecting to the spirit of air:
The week begins with exercises designed to help you clarify where you are in your life and environment right now, and your aims for the future. It provides an opportunity to discover your values and their relation to what you want to achieve. The values and ethics we hold create our personal sense of *self* and *identity*. Identifying that I value loyalty and integrity enables me to create a life that is in alignment with these qualities.

Water week's focus is on emotional clearing and connecting to the spirit of water:
Water is a symbol of intuition, trust and nurturing. It refreshes and renews. Life has similarities to a river in the way it ebbs, flows, twists and turns. Using the metaphor of a river, create your own River of Life Timeline. Portray the main events and turning points in your life by drawing a river that illustrates them. When you write down the meaning you gave each one, ask yourself 'is this true?' Be willing to replace it with a meaning that makes your life better.

After changing the meaning I've given to some of the events in my life I realize that, like the young swan, I've learned some truly valuable lessons. An important one is that *who I am is enough*, so that I can trust the way life flows.

Fire week concentrates on spiritual clearing and connecting with your spiritual self:
I particularly love the 'Facing Your Shadow' exercise, replacing *should* with *could*. While this may seem like a modest concept, it holds immense power for me as

I encounter my inner self critic. We can easily go through the day thinking that we *should* be doing this or that, and feeling guilty if we don't get round to it. When I change my internal dialogue to say I *could* do this or that, it feels like I have a choice and I feel empowered. It is a simple, powerful and effective technique.

Earth week connects us to the spirit of earth and physical clearing:
Earth week provides an opportunity to create a spiritual home for the soul in the form of an altar. For the small altar I created in my home I chose pebbles, crystals, driftwood and a candle. I carefully placed them on a shelf in the hallway where I can see them often as I pass by. At first this felt quite scary... as though I was putting my inner self on show for the world to see. To my amazement, friends and visitors commented on its beauty. Among my most prized possessions for my latest altar is a Tibetan singing bowl and hand painted mandala that my daughter brought back from her trip to Bali. I love her choice of gifts for me.

I highly recommend that you surround yourself with items that enthuse and uplift your spirit as a daily reminder of the life you want to achieve. This could be either a simple display or something more elaborate. Choose items that you love, that inspire you... a spiritual source, a photograph of someone you love or a favorite place with happy memories, crystals, sacred objects and a beautiful cloth. You could choose items that correspond with the four elements, such as a picture of the sky for the element of air, the sun or a candle for the element of fire, pebbles or a picture of a waterfall to represent water, and flowers or wood to symbolize the earth.

While following the 28 day program, I became my own 'Sacred Observer' by recording my thoughts and experiences each day in a Process Journal. This is a wonderfully easy way to become your own mentor. I've learned to embrace what I've achieved each day and release anything else. This bypasses my inner critic and fills me with positivity and a sense of accomplishment. I feel energized and charged with the momentum to create the life that I want.

Mind the gap

There are many challenges to be faced as we progress through life, ranging from the loss of youthfulness, perhaps a change in energy levels or health issues. Like other mothers, I experienced an 'empty nest' as my daughter moved away to university. At first I felt at a loss to know how best to move forward. However, I found myself provided with the perfect opportunity to focus on personal and spiritual fulfillment. Instinct guided me to become a Soul Coach, and this experience led me to study and explore other modalities, such as Hypnotherapy and Reiki.

The expansive toolbox I have developed has enabled me to offer my clients a much richer, fuller and more creative experience. By providing sacred space that feels safe, secure and non-judgmental, they can access their inner wisdom to create the life they desire.

Beauty, love and vision

In his book *Animal Speak,* the late Ted Andrews describes how the swan teaches us to awaken to the inner beauty in ourselves and others, regardless of outer appearances, and that when we are capable of this, we become a magnet to others. I see elements of the blossoming swan in both myself and my daughter. I feel honored and grateful when she tells me that her courage and confidence, as she explores the world physically and spiritually, stem from the lead she has taken from me and her Dad.

An important part of life and change is Love. In my own life, I have discovered love: love and acceptance of who and what I am, love of others – family and friends, love of music and much more. The wider Soul Coaching community is utterly vibrant and uplifting, filled with like-minded people. It challenges, educates and excites me. Above all, I have learned to face my fears so that they're not so scary anymore! I can even laugh about them. There will always be ups and downs in life, but nowadays the balance is definitely tipped in the favor of joy and living a full and happy life.

We are not the sum of our past. I know that when I have a strong vision and know it in my soul, I can go forward, allowing the past to dissolve. Soul Coaching has given me the tools to develop a consistent identity, to find my own inner swan, just as my daughter has. By holding a compelling vision of the future, even if it is of one simple thing, you too can create the life that you want, a life of your dreams.

∾

The Soul's Truth – a Daughter's Perspective

RACHEL PERRY

Man cannot discover new oceans
unless he has the courage to lose sight of the shore

—ANDRÉ GIDE

*M*y parents have always encouraged me to follow my dreams, and so I have been fortunate enough to study, work and backpack around the world. I know that wherever I am, they embrace me with wings of love. Sometimes I dream about looking into my future to see the steps I will take, so that I know where to focus my energies right now in this moment. I like the thought of being able to reflect back on how my life has evolved and see how my identity has been shaped. This makes me think of how the swan comes to live true to its identity by seeing its authentic reflection and finding its fellow swans.

The first step towards living the life of your dreams is to create a vision, and be willing to believe it will happen. Imagine you are on a road trip without a destination – you risk driving round in circles. Identifying your destination enables you to decide which route to take and how you will get there. Delving into the wisdom of your soul can help you not only discover your dreams, but also uncover a pathway to manifest them. When I am living the life of my dreams, I feel I am in the driver's seat.

One great thing about having the desire to explore your inner spirit or soul is discovering how to harness that power to create your own destiny. Accessing your inner wisdom is like the start of any other journey. If you don't know where to begin, ask yourself the question: "If I did know the answer, what would it be?" Use your imagination and trust in the messages that come to you!

As well as enjoying the thrill of working for a large company in the City of London, I'm also fascinated by the more esoteric path that my mother has followed. Her wisdom, support and voice of inspiration have fed my curiosity and helped to broaden my mind. I have also benefited from her healing capabilities too. It gives me enormous pleasure to witness her joy and contentment grow as she opens up her wings, taps into her creativity and shares her skills with the people drawn to her for coaching. We both share a natural desire to encourage and help others.

As we talked about Soul Coaching over the years, I saw a different, more spiritual side of Mum evolve, and wanted to explore that side of myself, though I'm not sure I ever actually *decided* to become a Soul Coach. You might be familiar with that feeling of 'it just kind of happened.' I've learned that when this sort of synchronicity occurs, my intuition and gut instinct are at work. When I hear this internal voice, I know I am listening to a message from my soul and there is a vital force at play.

My personal experience of Soul Coaching has transformed not only my vision of my future, it has also enhanced my experiences in the now, and how I reflect upon the past. Most of all, it has enriched the way I appreciate my loved ones and everyone around me.

Create your reality

Like the ugly duckling, each of us experiences our own unique version of reality. This is usually based on our individual perceptions of the significant people, events and influences throughout our life. From this our identity forms. However, it's the significance we give the experiences that determine our destiny, not just the experiences themselves. Just like in the River of Life Timeline exercise, *when we change the meaning we give to these events, we can change our life.*

I know if I forget to view situations through the eyes of others it can be difficult to understand their differing point of view. If we judge ourselves and our experience of reality as the status quo, it can also cause us to be judgmental and critical of other people. Denise Linn reminds us that *we don't know the whole story.*

We all have choices as to how we respond to any given situation and how we interpret our experience of it. When we choose to forgive our imperfections and accept ourselves with love, this is transmitted through our energy field. And as we become more empathetic and accepting of others, we also become more in tune and at one with our authentic selves.

The future belongs to those who believe in the beauty of their dreams.
Every time we feel the passion of our visions and dreams,
we awaken the creative spirit within us.

—TREE OF LIFE INSPIRATIONS©

Manifesting Your Dreams

Inside us all there is a wealth of opportunity, compassion and knowledge. Like the majestic swan, our thoughts are powerful. When we harness their magic and let our magnificence radiate, our dreams can become reality. As I clutter-cleared my mind, emotions, spirit and body on the 28 day program, it challenged me to reconsider my life and values.

Week one is devoted to the properties of Air:
The element of air represents transformation and inspiration by finding mental clarity.

A symbolic exercise for me was creating my first collage of what I wanted to manifest over the coming year. Soul Coaching collages work in an almost magical way because they focus on the *feelings* that achieving the goal you desire will bring. They capture messages from your soul and are a visual manifestation of your purpose, giving form to the formless, and creating positive, supportive energy.

Begin by setting your intention. Close your eyes and ask your soul *what is the purpose of this collage?* Be aware of images, spontaneous insights and feelings that arise. Let your intuition guide you to choose the type of collage you want to create. It might be to affirm your mission or purpose in life, to overcome a challenge you're facing, or gain focus on the year ahead.

Cut out pictures from magazines or any other images you have at hand. Allow your creativity and intuition to flow. Narrow down your selection, then arrange each item onto a poster board. When you are happy with your chosen items, glue them into place. Add any embellishments, words or drawings that help you express the messages from your soul.

Prop the completed collage in front of you and spend some time absorbing the insights or messages that emerge; use all your senses to reinforce how it feels to have achieved your goals. In doing so, the images serve as affirmations to your conscious mind that will anchor into your subconscious – the subconscious doesn't discriminate between real and imagined events. Look out for and have conviction in any hints or signals that will help manifest your dreams. Remember: *where intention goes energy flows.*

Finally, position your collage somewhere you can see it regularly to allow its energy to reinforce your intentions. You could also scan it to use as a screen saver, or copy and shrink it to carry in your wallet.

Week two is devoted to the properties of Water:
The element of water is fresh and cleansing, it symbolizes the flow of life.

I particularly love the simplicity and effectiveness of keeping a Gratitude Journal – one of the exercises in water week. At the end of each day, write down anything that has crossed your path for which you are truly grateful. It is often the simplest things that give me the most joy. A beaming smile on the face of a stranger that contagiously creeps across my face too, the sun shining bright in the sky, the first signs of a planted seed beginning to sprout its green leaves, or a kind word from a friend that takes me by surprise.

By focusing your attention on the aspects of your day for which you are grateful, you become mindful of them and attract more of them into your life. This is self-perpetuating – as you experience more gratitude, you feel happier. Your happiness is infectious and so the cycle continues.

There are no isolated acts… emotions, attitudes and behavior
travel from person to person, infecting everyone they touch.

—DAVID HAMILTON

Week three is devoted to the properties of Fire:
Fire week provides an opportunity to confront fears and take action. It's about learning to live in the present moment and embracing your passions in life.

When I graduated from university at the age of 22, having been on the treadmill of education that had laid out my path until then, I felt somewhat daunted by the breadth of options available to me. Unsure of my next destination, I felt uncertain about what the future would hold for me. I didn't have any particular expectations or sense of what the *life of my dreams* would look like. Although happy with the life choices I had made before and since, an element of trepidation about my future remained with me. I hoped to tackle this during a guided Soul Journey.

The Soul Journey began with a guided relaxation – meandering along a forest path before stepping into a wooden hut. I was introduced to this fear, which represented itself as a dark, ethereal figure. My Soul Coach guided me to shrink the figure down in size until it transformed into a ball of shimmering golden light. The light expanded to fill the entire room with its beautiful luminosity. Since then, my sense of inner calm and innate trust in my intuition and ability to judge what is right for me has grown in strength… and continues to develop.

Week four is devoted to the properties of Earth:
The element of earth represents grounding and nurturing yourself.

Spending time outdoors and feeling the nourishing energy of the earth replenishes me. I love the feeling of cool, springy grass on the bare soles of my feet. Watching the clouds float gently across the sky and hearing the breeze rustle through the trees calms my mind, slowing the pace of inner dialogue.

To ground a new vision of your future, imagine it is one year from now and write yourself a letter describing how fabulous the preceding year has been. Include all the good things that have happened. Write it as if it has actually happened and make it as realistic as possible. As Denise Linn says, *as you feel it you become it.*

This technique is most effective when you choose a few areas on which to focus (don't make it so vast that it is impossible to achieve). Write it in an upbeat way and include as much detail as you can so it feels real and tangible. This is an excellent way to gain insight into how you will feel once you have made the changes you have identified. When you have finished your letter, meet with a trusted friend and describe to them how wonderful the past year has been. Make your story as realistic and vibrant as you can.

Another simple way to synchronize with the rhythms of nature is to rise with the sun and go to sleep as darkness falls.

Trust that you already know the answer

In my experience, the answers we are seeking lie within ourselves. When we take the time that we deserve, to be still and be open to our soul within, the answers we are looking for will flow to the surface. Resolve to be a *finder* rather than a seeker.

Close your eyes and you will see clearly.
Cease to listen and you will hear.

−TAOIST MEDITATION

Getting to know your soul can feel like the beginning of the rest of your life. With practice, you can learn to trust the messages you hear from the depths of your soul as it shares its divinity from within. Feel safe in the knowledge that the future will take care of itself; like attracts like and when you emanate positivity, so it will be drawn to you. Once you begin to believe that you have the power to create the future of your dreams and truly know that you are safe, you will look at everything that comes your way in a more favorable light, and look forward with excitement to living the life of your dreams.

Bibliography

Gide, André. Adapted from *Les faux-monnayeurs*. La Nouvelle Revue Française, 1925.
Hamilton, David. *The Contagious Power of Thinking*. Hay House, 2011.
Tree of Life Inspirations © Copyright Tree of Life Inspirations UK. www.treeol.co.uk

Trusting Your Intuition

AFFIRMATION: *My life is truly guided.*

Listen with your heart and act on your instincts. Trust that you are being guided, as the messages you are receiving are in your highest good. Follow the nudges from Spirit.

ALISSA IIDA
Las Vegas, Nevada, USA

ALISSA IIDA'S CHILDHOOD was filled with questions about how the world functioned. She wanted to know the 'why's' behind every statement. Thus, although she began her spiritual quest at a young age, she did not realize it at the time.

She loved studying and the academic world became her life. She received her Bachelor of Arts and Master of Arts degrees in European Languages & Literature, became a National Board Certified Teacher in World Languages Other than English, earned a Master of Science degree in Counseling and is currently working on a PhD in Metaphysics. She has been a Spanish and English as a Second Language teacher and counselor for 15 years.

Soon, her academics were not enough to fulfill her. This is when her true quest for spiritual knowledge began to blossom. Alissa has been blessed to have the opportunity to study with Doreen Virtue, Sonia Choquette, Denise Linn, Debra Katz, Kim O'Neill, and many others. Her certifications include: Angel Therapy Practitioner® and Medium, Six Sensory, Soul Coach & Past Life Regression Coach, SoulCollage, Chakradance, Reiki Master and Akashic Records.

She finally discovered her life purpose – to become a Women's Life Guidance Coach. Alissa coaches people from all over the world. Many of her clients are people who have been sexually abused and are still learning to heal from their traumatic experiences.

Alissa is also an inspirational speaker, sharing her healing journey of being a sexual abuse survivor. Contact her at angelicmeditations@gmail.com and check out her website at www.lovingyourselfwithangels.com

Loving Yourself with Angels

ALISSA IIDA

By communicating with the angels through your own heart,
you too can heal your wounds. It is time to let go, be free and live your life.

"*What?!* I'm not going to Heaven *or* Hell did you say? According to whom?" As a child attending a parochial school, the nuns often mentioned that there's no place for a soul if it hadn't been baptized. Oh no! I was going to be in limbo after I died, never ascending to Heaven. What a frightening thought for a nine year old! I would never be able to fly with the angels.

Fortunately, Sister Nelita was a sweet nun, with the most kind and gentle spirit. She had the soul of a nurturing mother whose love flowed endlessly. Being a timid child, I did not have the courage to do most things. Sister Nelita *saved* me. She was *my* angel. This gracious angel took the notion to take care of me, to watch me grow and to support me. I am forever grateful for this blessing. I helped Sister Nelita every day after school and this is where my journey of the most important lessons in my life began, learning what it meant to truly love myself.

As a child, for several years, I was molested. Fear aroused many emotions: shame, embarrassment, resentment, anger, sadness, despise, but most of all, guilt – guilt laid on thick for something that I did not want, do, or cause. Because I was threatened with violence if I had spoken up, the sexual abuse continued. My parents had no idea. In their minds, they believed that it was a basic case of separation anxiety every time I was dropped off. Fortunately, we moved away and it never happened again. Unfortunately, I was still traumatized and these emotions continued into my adult life.

Being molested and feeling unworthy had caused me to examine my core beliefs. My beliefs were: I am a good person, but why do bad things happen to good people? I should not feel guilty, but why do I? I feel so dirty, how could I ever feel clean again? A multitude of questions bombarded me like rocks falling off a cliff all at once. Then, a prayer to the angels led me on a very different path. You see, I had not asked the angels for help while being molested. I thought that they would have also seen me as a 'dirty' and 'unworthy' child. But all I needed to do was to ask for help.

As someone who often pondered, "Who am I?" I was to discover that Soul

Coaching helps you to speak from your soul and allows you to be your true, authentic self without fear, doubt or denial. Denise describes this program as "a process that takes you to your own spiritual source and helps you find meaning and sacredness in your every day life. It allows you to take an honest look at yourself and your life, face fear, release old negative patterns, get motivated, and step boldly and joyously into your future." Having permission to belong in this scared space was one of my first journeys towards accepting my whole self. Through Denise Linn's Soul Coaching program, I have learned many valuable life lessons. Let me share my journey with the angels and how they taught me to completely love me for me.

There are four elements that exist in Soul Coaching (Air, Water, Fire and Earth) that correlate with the whole being: mental, emotional, spiritual and physical. During mental cleansing week, or Air week, I decided to declutter my house, so I hired a professional organizer. After decluttering boxes, clothes, and other stuff, the house had become even more of a sacred space. A sense of accomplishment had taken over. Then, feelings of guilt and shame arose. What happened? I'm supposed to be feeling like a million dollars, but why don't I? Well, due to the constant organizing, 'stuff was coming up'. Not knowing where to turn, I closed my eyes, sat in silence and called on my angels. As I called upon these wonderful beings of insight, my heart filled with bright, white light, a sense of calm and most of all, pure innocent love – love so carefully woven into my heart that I could just cry it all out – and I did.

Air week cleansed my mind, leaving so much clarity within me. The 'stuff' that was coming up was related to letting go. How do we let go of the past? Everyone's journey happens in its own Divine timing. I asked my angels, "What do I need to learn here?" I learned that hanging onto the past would not help me, so why hold on? I needed to learn how to forgive others, but most of all, to forgive myself.

Continuing on with Air week, I realized that I needed to *accept* the fact that sexual abuse did occur, but that I did not have to carry the weight of that burden. What good does holding on do? The only person suffering is me! I was tired of feeling 'dirty'. Next, a sweet whisper sounded in my ear. An angel murmured, "Surrender my child. You are a child of God. You are not guilty. You need not be ashamed. You need not be embarrassed, for we, the angels, will hold your hands for eternity. You are one of us and you are so very loved." With that message, the heaviest weight on my shoulders catapulted into the Heavens, and I was free! Once I released these negative patterns, I forgave the person, in spirit, who molested me. But most of all, I gave myself permission to forgive myself. With this blessing, I have accepted that to love one's self is to forgive one's self.

While learning how to forgive, I also learned how to shift into a new paradigm of thinking as I moved on to Water Week. Water detoxes your body, purifying it and allowing it to be a container of good health. While growing up in Hawaii, I played in the ocean almost every day – splashing, swimming, sinking my toes into the sand and just having fun as a child should. The ocean would pick me up, caress my skin and make all my worries disappear. My inner child jumped with joy and delight. Now that I had learned how to surrender and let go of my awful past by accepting it, it was time for my inner child to come out to play. My personality switched from bashful to extroverted. My fears had disappeared and a total new 'me' emerged. Incredible transformation occurred. All the past emotions I wrestled with had now been released. With the energy of the past dispersed, it was time to move boldly forward. How exciting! I was free! Free! Free! Free! No more guilt! No more shame! No more embarrassment! How wonderful to be able to walk with my head held high and proud, leading myself forward with a renewed spirit, with my angels always nearby.

Angels come in many shapes and forms. Whenever I'm near the ocean, I believe that the angels are present with me, especially when something magical happens. For example, if I've been longing to see a dolphin and a dolphin shows his fin out of the ocean, or I see a gorgeous sparkle on the seashore that no other grain of sand has, or maybe there is a dog that is just passing by and gives me a nudge to say hello… You may think that these things are just ordinary occurrences, but in my eyes, I am so grateful for these signs of love and joy from the angels.

I often look for signs in the clouds. Once there was this huge, magical cloud in the shape of an angel, another time, in the shape of angel wings. They were the beautiful, majestic, wondrous shapes of these higher beings. Pay attention to what you see in the clouds. Is it in the shape of an angel, their wings, or perhaps your favorite animal? You will be in wonder as you begin paying attention to the signs all around you. What a marvelous world we live in! Pure magnificence. On the other hand, when you are out in the open air, you may see their signs as a quick flash in the sky, a beautiful sunset or sunrise, or a beautiful baby giving you a smile. If you pay close attention, you may see angels everywhere, and you can ask your angels for anything.

Once, I really wanted to fly first class on a flight, but on the Internet, it said that first class was not available. I told myself, "I don't believe what I'm seeing. Let's go check it out at the airport." So I did. While at the kiosk, I said, "Angels, do your magic. Archangel Michael, make room for me." I was walking in the unseen realm called faith. I thanked the angels and Archangel Michael and pushed the buttons on the kiosk. It said, "No first class seats available. Continue." Well, not taking no for an answer, like a mischievous child, I pushed the upgrade button anyway. Not to my surprise, it now said, "One seat available in first class." Yes angels! I knew that you could do it. I said a prayer of gratitude and appreciation. Often times our beliefs get in the way. By changing negative thinking patterns to positive ones, we can create absolute miracles in our lives. For within the word 'impossible' are the words, 'I-(a)m-possible.'

Sometimes we don't believe that we deserve good things, and this ugly thought process comes from not being able to love ourselves. When you are able to love yourself, blessings of abundance will drop into your lap like magic.

What do you think of when you think of abundance? I used to think that abundance was about money because my family was poor. My mother was divorced before I turned three. Children of divorced parents in my generation were treated like outcasts. To internalize these feelings as a child was just awful. Many times during my childhood, I felt alone, scared, and most of all, unworthy.

I have learned that when I love myself, so many things that once seemed impossible can be changed to be possible. As I think about love, I also think about the love and support that the angels have given me. I have been able to be abundant in a continuous stream of love; a sea full of emotions; wonder beyond amazement while traveling the world; being surrounded with trustworthy friends and family; and most all, an abundance of laughter. My angels have a sense of humor and make me giggle all the time. They are pure comedians. One day, I was driving on the freeway and I thought to myself, "Oh my! I'd better stop speeding because I don't want another speeding ticket." Before I could step on the brakes, a van sped in front of me, and his license plate said something like, "SLWDWN." I laughed so hard, and then thanked the angels for watching over my safety.

Since releasing the 'dirty' emotions, my inner child wants to play all the time. She is free! So free! To be able to laugh freely has helped to heal my wounded soul. The bandage has been torn off, tossed away, and finally, I *am* alive. What an exhilarating feeling! By communicating with the angels through your own heart, you too can heal your wounds. It is time to let go, be free and live your life. Imagine a life filled with laughter, friendships, family that you adore, and so much more. Remember that you are the Master of Your Life. Take control and plunge into the excitement of life. Life is there, waiting for you.

Sit in silence, call on your angels and communicate with your heart. What does your heart really want? Are you already living it or are you allowing things to stand in your way? Make a plan, execute it and enjoy what's coming. Yes, you will have ups and downs in any situation, but remember it's all in *how* you handle these situations. Always remember to love yourself and to speak from love. With love in the air, how could you not succeed? It's your life and now's the time to show off the real, authentic you. Go for it! You may say, "But I'm afraid." Acknowledging your fears is one of the greatest accomplishments that you can achieve. If I did it, so can you.

Soul Coaching speaks about fears in Fire Week. Denise Linn says "A fear named is a fear tamed." Why are we so afraid to get out of our comfort zone? You may say "What will people think of me?" My question to you is, "What does it matter?" It's your life. I used to be so paranoid about how people would react to me. I have learned that it doesn't matter. It's my life and I'm willing to live. No more excuses.

Many people on their deathbed report one major regret – they lived their lives as someone else had wanted them to live. If they could have lived their life over, they would have done things differently. They would have lived their own life with no one else's permission. Take risks! What do you have to lose? If you're not willing to take those risks, you're only regret might be "What if...?"

The number one fear for many people is public speaking, and it's one of my greatest fears. But in order to share my story, I must be heard. One day, you will hear my whole story. My fear was, "How do I speak about my sexual abuse to the world?" Then, I remembered that I could always ask the angels for help. I said a prayer, "I'm afraid. Please help me to share my story with the world." Because of the angels, I have mustered up the courage to speak up about being a survivor of abuse and the steps that I have taken in order to overcome my challenges. I have already told a group of women my story and it was one of the most healing moments ever. With the angels' help, I have learned to overcome another fear and to live a full life.

When I learned to not judge others by worrying about what they would think about me, I accepted my own self without judgments. It's true that the only time we judge others is when we are judging ourselves. About a year ago, I gained a lot of weight due to my new position as a counselor. Instead of standing or walking around the classroom as a teacher, now I was stationary at a desk. I often woke up with these comments, "Arrghh! I hate my body. How did I put on so much weight? Why can't I lose it? The scale *has* to be wrong." It took me many months to realize that I was doing more harm than good to my body. Feeding your body negative messages leaves your body in a state of desperation.

I finally realized that in order to lose the weight, I had to *love* my body. It has been one of my most difficult challenges as I fell into depression, especially when people made comments such as, "You're chubby now. Oh! You've gained some weight. I can tell you've put on a few, extra pounds." How could people be so cruel? But they weren't intentionally being mean, just honest.

In the spiritual world, we know that counselors and persons in similar professions take on other people's energies and if you're not careful, often, the result is weight gain. This weight serves as protection against foreign energies such as people's problems. As a Soul Coach, I needed to reflect back to see what would work for me. Thus, a new routine began in the morning in front of my mirror. First, I would pick an angel card from one of my angel decks and it would give me a message such as, "You are beautiful just the way you are," or "Nurture yourself today." The angels gave me permission to love myself, because I had not been ready to give myself permission. Next, I'd say, "I'm fat and I love my fat! I love my fat body!" My motto every morning became "I absolutely love and adore my fat body."

Guess what? I began to feel lighter, my clothes began fitting again, and before I knew it, there was more happiness than depression. The next time I stepped onto the scale, I had lost five pounds. Now that's progress! I realized that in order to love yourself, you must love your body. You must take care of your body by eating healthy, doing exercise and getting enough rest. Thus, I gave up soda, began dance classes and am more aware of my eating habits. I can't say that I have lost all of my extra weight, but I'm *okay* with it. I now wake up every morning loving myself instead of hating my body. I took action to change my quality of life and the results have been amazing.

During Earth Week in Soul Coaching, one of the goals is for you to focus on the physical nature of your environment. I looked up to the Heavens and asked the angels, "What action step can I take to nourish my soul?" The angels replied, "Create a scared space." So I created a dream altar. On this altar, I have placed my vision boards and items that are close to my heart.

I have achieved all of my dreams so far. I have traveled to many foreign countries, taught language and dance in China and Poland, and have studied with my favorite authors. As soon as one of my dreams has been realized, I remove the old item from my altar and replace it with a new dream. My new dreams include purchasing a flat in Paris, becoming a #1 New York Times Bestselling author, and teaching seminars around the world, traveling first class and making a minimum six-figure income. My greatest dream is to help thousands of people to heal their 'wounded self' – to show that they can sincerely love themselves too. By creating my altar, I am reminded of what I love and what gives me energy to continue being happy, and most of all, to remind myself that as long as I love myself, I am able to love others with all of my heart. As my mother often told me while growing up, "I love you with all my big heart." And my response would be, "And I love you with all my little heart."

Receiving from Angels

AFFIRMATION: Shimmering wings of angels embrace me with love.

Blessings from above are showering over your life. Angels are real, and their presence is near — they are only a thought away. Messengers from the Creator, they come to you with immense blessings and love. All is well. Spread your wings and soar!

A couple of Denise Linn's books are on my dream altar. Denise has been a mentor on how to love one's self as she demonstrates unconditional love. She once held a contest on the most popular social media website. Denise would gift a goat to a non-profit international organization to the person's comment that received the most 'likes' on her or his quote. I prayed to the angels and asked them to help me win. Bring it on! Guess what? I won! Woohoo! Denise donated a goat in honor of my name and I also matched her gift. She was so touched by the gesture that she expressed tears of gratitude. I am extremely grateful for Denise's authenticity and being able to learn one of the most important lessons in my life, to also believe in myself. Dreams do come true. So never ever give up on your dreams.

Self-love is one of the most difficult lessons that I have had to learn. It has not always been easy. As a sexually abused child, I did not know how to love my own self because of being traumatized. Without the help of the angels' answered prayers,

I would not be here today as my spirit had withered and died during the abuse. Through my journey, I have realized that true love comes from within yourself. When you are able to love your own self, you are able to love others. When you see love in others, there is no judgment, nor harm. When you are able to reach this higher level of consciousness, and you are able to love with your whole heart, you 'see' people for who they are; but most of all, you are able to accept them as they are as people. Creating this type of love is one of the highest energies that you could ever experience.

Remember to love yourself, nurture yourself, accept yourself, and most importantly, to truly become your authentic self. Ask the angels to guide you on your path and they will hold your hands for eternity too. Listen carefully to your angels. With their messages, you will be able to connect with your heart, love yourself more each day, and most importantly, heal your wounds so that you may move courageously forward in your life.

Discovering Self-Love with the Angels
In this meditation, you will discover the pure love and essence of the angels. Play some relaxing music and then record yourself saying the following meditation.

Sit in a comfortable position and take a couple of deep breaths. Imagine yourself in a land filled with beautiful colored flowers, a nearby brook that whispers as it passes over the smooth rocks in the water on a warm, sunny day. Next to the creek is some mud on the grass. The mud is clean, soft and waiting for you to caress it. Feel the texture of the healing clay. The Earth Angels are preparing the mud to help you heal. Soon, you will be picking up a clump of mud for each part of you that you would like to replenish. It's time to grab a clump of mud. For the first clump, say, "This clump will help me to heal my heart," and place that clump on your heart or wherever you feel necessary. Then, pick up the next clump and say, "I am beautiful. I deserve all good things. I am worthy," and place the clump on your chest. Do this for each part of yourself that needs to feel whole again. Continue on until you feel complete.

You have now placed all of the mud clay on your body. Next, take a couple of deep breaths and imagine bright rays of sunshine shining upon your body. You feel the warmth of the sun, but it does not burn you. You are safe. The Fire Angels help to break your resistance. The warm rays bake the clay on your body until the mud begins cracking. The cracking symbolizes all the old patterns being released into the universe. As each part cracks, your body is transforming into a new Self. You are whole. Old, negative thinking patterns are broken, making room only for the positive. You are beautiful. You are amazing. You are unique. You are love. You love yourself oh so very much. The angels hug you for a few seconds. Feel the warmth of the angels surround you. You are healed. Your spirit is free. Sit in the warmth for a few more minutes.

Remember that you are a gentle, kind soul with so much love – love to give yourself first so that you may love others even more so. Walk over to the creek. You will slowly enter the water about knee deep. If you're afraid to step into the water, sit on the edge of the brook and place your feet into the water. Allow the cool water to run over your body, cleansing off the mud, and rejuvenating your spirit. The Water Angels fill your spirit with an endless flow of love. Continue washing the mud off with your hands. If you're feeling brave, go deeper into the water and sink your body into the refreshing, moving water until all the mud has been cleaned off. The water feels so good. The Water Angels are taking a dip into the water and cleansing themselves too. They speak to you about Self-Love. What are they saying? What do they look like? What message did they give to you? Only loving messages come from the angels. Which special message did they whisper to you?

It's time to dry off. Begin walking in the garden, smelling the beautiful flowers and slowly, you feel the water drops falling off your body. You feel the Air Angels' hands wiping your body down. With each wipe, they fill you with joy and happiness. Look at the majestic trees, gorgeous flowers, green plants and shimmering creek. Imagine these creatures having a conversation with you. What special message did they share with you? Enjoy your wonderful messages from the Air Angels and nature spirits. Know that your spirit is free, whole and amazing. Slowly shake your feet and arms. Come out of trance, and when you're ready, open your eyes.

You have now experienced a journey with the angels and the four elements. Remember to always love yourself and to call on the angels at any time. Get a piece of paper and write down your messages. Now step joyously into your future by loving your authentic self!

Awakening Ancient Wisdom

AFFIRMATION: *Deep inner knowing*
is emerging within me.

The wisdom of the ages dwells within
you. It is arising now. The chalice
of wisdom is being offered to you.
Pay attention to the coincidences,
signs, and synchronicities around you.
Profound enlightenment is
growing within you, even if
you are not aware of it

LESLIE JACKSON
Woodland Park, Colorado, USA

LESLIE JACKSON IS passionate about the process of self-discovery. She creates a space for people to connect to their heart experience of the Divine, to explore and express their life purpose, and create and live their best life. She draws on her experience as a mixed-media artist, photographer, poet, writer, and teacher to lead fun and creative 'playshops', study groups, and women's circles. Leslie is also a gifted intuitive, and her clients have come to appreciate the 'something extra' that often comes with their individual healing and coaching work.

Leslie is an ordained Interfaith Minister and founder of Kaleidoscope Village, Center for Integrative Healing in Colorado Springs, Colorado. All of her work reflects the spiritual nature of our human experience. She holds a Master of Science degree in Holistic Ministries and has been busy learning and earning multiple certifications for a variety of healing modalities including Usui Reiki, drumming, dream work, card reading, life coaching, spiritual direction, and Soul Coaching. All of these serve to enrich the kaleidoscope of self-discovery opportunities that Leslie's clients enjoy.

Leslie and her husband have been married for 25 years. Together they have two amazing and spirited young-adult children, a variety of pound puppies and kitties, and a home in the Colorado Rocky Mountains.

For inspiration for your best-lived life, visit Leslie's website and blog at www.MyKaleidoscopeVillage.com.

Oracle Cards: Secrets and Soul Whispers

LESLIE JACKSON

One of my greatest pleasures is drawing a card for the day. I love their uplifting and inspirational messages, and I value their gentle, introspective guidance.

Don't you think there is something magical, enchanting, and even precious about a secret? What if that secret is all about you? Even better, what if it's all about the wondrous, loving and happy you... all the *best* parts of you? And what if the secret is a magical key that unlocks all the joy and beauty of your best-lived life? To me, oracle cards are like the treasure box that holds those secret, magical keys. Each picture, phrase or word invites you to open a door and step into those best parts, the ones you may be out of touch with, unconscious of, and unable to see.

In days gone by, we've consulted shamans, sages, seers, priestesses, masters and elders for answers to the questions of our lives. The word oracle has its roots in the Latin *oraculum* meaning 'divine announcement'. In antiquity, an oracle was 'the agency or medium of a god' and in the Holy Bible, an oracle is the 'Word of God'. One of the most well-known and fascinating references to oracles in history was the oracle of Apollo at Delphi in ancient Greece. This oracle was unique in that it was a woman, called the Pythoness or Pythia, and people came for miles to ask for her guidance.

Many of us seek this guidance still, though perhaps less dramatically than the Greek citizens. If you are like me, you are always asking questions, examining your choices and feelings, and exploring your ideas and actions. Where does this yearning for answers come from? What is this deep place inside of us that is constantly seeking? How do we create a life of meaning and purpose?

I had been asking the life-purpose question for some time. It seems I'm a little bit scattered when it comes to my interests and gifts. One minute I'm logical and methodical and efficiently ticking detail-oriented tasks off my to-do list, and in the next I'm doing oracle card readings, leading art and photography 'playshops', and coaching my clients on their healing paths. I read somewhere that I'm what they call a "Renaissance Soul". Of course, some call it unfocused, lacking in commitment, or even lazy, though I think I prefer Renaissance Soul. Why did I lack direction? One of my dearest friends has known what she wanted for years, has gone after it, and every day gets up and goes to it. Good for her; but why did this sense of purpose continue to elude me? In searching for the answers, I recognized that there were quiet little whispers when I sat still long enough to listen, and I discovered oracle cards are a wonderful tool to connect me to those whispers.

Our soul, or 'higher self', is the built-in guidance system for our being. It is the place of knowing within us, that fathomless place where we touch God and God touches us. The soul is the essence of who we are as spiritual beings. It is, in fact, where *all* the answers lie. The sages and teachers have always understood that the answers are within us rather than outside of us. Of course, we sometimes need help hearing the soul's messages and discerning what they mean in our own lives. When I went searching for answers about my purpose, they came in signs, symbols and metaphors. These pictures, as it happens, are how our souls speak to us.

Incidentally, as you might expect from someone writing about oracle cards and the whispers of the soul, I selected an oracle card before writing this chapter. The card I drew from *The Tarot of Transformation* deck, by Willow Arlenea and Jasmin Lee Cori, indicated 'Joyous Flow'. It signifies contentment, not forcing or pushing, just being in the joyous flow of the process. These are wise words indeed, and when I find myself struggling, or trying too hard, I am reminded to remain in the joyous flow.

I considered joining Denise Linn for her Soul Coaching certification for almost two years before I enrolled. I had been knocking around the World Wide Web trying to find a Life Coaching school to complete my certification. When I started taking coaching courses in early 2001, a whole new world opened up to me. Suddenly, I was discovering answers to long-forgotten questions. The more I learned and the more I coached others, the more I discovered about myself. As is often the way, once I stepped forward onto the path of coaching, connections and synchronicities occurred, sometimes at astonishing speeds. Through a conversation about relationships with a coworker, I was guided to a book. While I was reading that book, I saw an article in a magazine about the author of the same book. That article talked about an idea, and I found a place to meet people with similar ideas. I was invited to a class, and while I was there, I discovered other books and authors and ideas, and on it went.

In this age of certifications, and the push for a piece of paper to give 'credibility', I was feeling some pressure to do that for my coaching business. You see, I never actually finished all my coaching courses at the well-known online school I was enrolled in. I wasn't interested in becoming a corporate coach, and at that time, my school required both life coaching and corporate coaching classes in order to graduate. I finished all my life coaching requirements, but not the rest. Hence, no handy piece of paper to tell the world that what I have to offer has value.

My soul, however, was deeply interested in pursuing a spiritual path to coaching. I couldn't make sense of the idea of the human being separate from Spirit, and I didn't want to shy away from the 'God Conversation'. I wanted to *go there*, so to speak. I wanted to connect with people on a deeply meaningful level. When I came upon the Soul Coaching Certification Course, I knew that was the answer. Reading about the course itself, and then reading all the testimonials filled something inside of me that I hadn't realized was empty. Strangely enough, the piece of paper was the least of my concerns, though I now have one and it is beautiful!

However, I wasn't ready just yet. I was busy working on my graduate degree in Holistic Ministries. As my education progressed, I experienced an incredible opening in my heart and my world. I explored healing modalities such as energy healing, sound and light therapies, and psychoneuroimmunology (trust science to give us a big word for the mind-body connection), and opened my heart and mind to new ideas about God, spirituality, and faith. I learned to lead drum circles, and discovered another way to positively impact people's lives. A friend invited me to join her for a First Degree Reiki workshop and I was hooked. I worked my way to Reiki Master and I now enjoy teaching.

I discovered I have a deep intuitive gift that is helpful in my clients' healing processes. In my work, I have also found that using oracle cards is one way to mine the soul for gems of wisdom and guidance, and my clients love this process. I will draw a card before the session starts and I let it sit in my conscious awareness as we talk. Recently, I drew a card from a gorgeous deck called *Mystic Art Medicine Oracle Cards* by Cher Lyn with that morning's client in mind. The card was 'Love', and it depicted an ethereal rendering of the Christ's face and the Tree of Life. This particular client is very devout and bears beautiful witness to the love of Jesus Christ. The story she shared with me that morning involved a near-death experience and her meeting Jesus. Among the other important details she shared was a moment when, as she described in her words, "I looked into the eyes of Jesus."

At the end of her session, I showed her the card I had drawn, for I felt she may resonate with it in a powerful way. I didn't tell her that the artist's intent was to depict the Cosmic Christ. I like to keep quiet and allow people to discover what they will in the cards. She saw the Tree of Life first, and then saw the eyes of Jesus as painted by the artist. She spoke very quietly when she told me those eyes were familiar to her and she had seen them before. When I told her of the artist's intent, she could only nod and hold the card to her heart. Images can offer such profound connection and meaning for us.

It was during one of my personal readings that I realized it was time for Soul Coaching. The question I was asking had to do with clarity about my purpose (again). All signs pointed to California. When I received my registration packet for the Soul Coaching Certification Program, it included the 'Success' card from Denise Linn's *Soul Coaching Oracle Cards* deck. I remember thinking that it affirmed everything I hoped for in pursuing this certification. So, in April, 2011, I set out by myself on a road trip to Denise Linn's Summerhill Ranch. It was a cold and snowy day as I left Colorado and drove into a foggy and rainy Utah. In Nevada, the wind blew away the clouds, and I finally made my way into the sun in southern California. The drive was blissful and relaxing, and served to get me into slow-down mode. When I left home, I had felt as though I needed to breathe, as if something in my daily life was constricting and uncomfortable.

As I drove, I felt this constriction fall away. Of course, I had to stop at Disneyland, a childhood (and adulthood) favorite. There's nothing like a little "Yo Ho" and "Small World" to lighten your spirit. Then I treated myself to a night at a lovely little cottage by the sea in Cambria, where I watched the seals on Moonstone Beach for hours. Though I missed my family, this alone-time was a blessing. I needed the rhythms of the changing weather, the rushing waves, and the solitude. As I watched the sun sink into the sea, I knew that I was exactly where I needed to be in that moment. The next morning, I drove to the meeting place and met Denise and the ladies who would become my Soul Sisters.

My time at Summerhill was like time-out-of-time. Every day there were opportunities to commune with nature, to learn and listen, and to connect on a soul-deep level with people, many from other countries and cultures. I felt so enriched by the harmony we created as we ate together, laughed and cried together, and journeyed together. I left Summerhill a changed person. I knew the cards had been right on. I was ready to listen to the whispers of my soul and unlock the secrets of my best life. One of my favorite memories of that magical time was the evening when I took an oracle deck into the neighboring Wildflower Room with two of my Soul Sisters. I had offered to do readings for them, and we enjoyed a very precious few hours together. I was honored by their trust as we found common ground in our connections and stories. Together we searched for meaningful treasure in the wisdom of the cards.

For years, I have been collecting both Tarot and oracle card decks, always drawn to their beautiful artwork. I look for decks that tap into feminine wisdom, worlds of folklore and myth and messengers from Spirit. I love losing myself in the imagery, and gradually discovering its mysteries. I am attracted to positive, enchanting and poetic words, as well. One of my greatest pleasures is drawing a card for the day. I love their uplifting and inspirational messages, and I value their gentle, introspective guidance. Several years ago when my daughter started middle school, we drew from a deck with affirmations every morning before school to help her with the extreme anxiety she was experiencing. She said it helped her feel more positive, even if she couldn't remember the exact words of the affirmation. It also gave us a beautiful way to start each day together.

If you are interested in the history of oracle cards or the Tarot, there are many resources available. I will give you a fast-forward version here. Today's Tarot cards are the descendants of playing cards, which first appeared in the Tang Dynasty in the 9th century. The origin of the Tarot is often debated, with some believing they are derived from ancient Egyptian mystery schools, China, or the 'gypsies'. Rachel Pollack, in her book *Tarot Wisdom: Spiritual Teachings and Deeper Meanings*, states "… the original pictures come from well-known scenes, primarily religious, found in Northern Italy from the late Middle Ages." The pictures she refers to are found in the 15th century Visconti-Sforza, a nearly complete deck that has since been revived, and is the earliest-known Tarot. The decks were used as a parlor game, but it seems the true purpose and intent was divination. The Tarot typically includes 78 cards and is a complex system of archetypes, symbolism and meaning. Oracle decks are similar in that they may include all of those things, but they can vary in number of cards, structure and theme, depending on the intent of the author and artist.

Oracle cards, independent of the Tarot, were used in 19th century France. Madame Marie Lenormand was a professional fortune teller, active in Paris for over 40 years. She rose to popularity among the French nobility using a deck of oracle cards she had devised on her own. Though less lengthy than the history of the Tarot, it is clear that oracle cards have been used for over 200 years. The last 50 or so years have seen a resurgence of oracle cards with a variety of influences. My favorite decks offer a spiritual view that uplifts and enlightens, and I enjoy using decks for meditation, affirmation and insight.

When working with the language of the soul, it is important that you allow yourself to remain open and receptive. You can create blockages when you are tired, distracted, overwhelmed, or afraid. These blockages prevent you from hearing the whispers from within. One of the first things to consider is your intention. You can approach any sign, symbol, animal messenger, dream, oracle card, or Tarot card with the attitude of curiosity and wonder. Remember that these are attempts from your soul to be heard and understood, and the messages are for your highest good. But, when you draw a card, or create a spread with multiple cards, how do you discern their meaning? In other words, how do you *know*? It is, after all, answers we are seeking, right?

To start, make it your intention to create meaning from a place of love and purpose. Bless your cards and infuse them with loving energy. You can invite Spirit or your ancestors, angels and spirit guides to be present for you. Then look closely at the words and pictures and see what stands out for you. *Trust your soul to know what to show you.* There is usually an accompanying book or booklet that tells you the meanings according to the author of the deck. Sometimes these are helpful, but remember that the cards have messages that are personal and especially for you. It is best to discern your own meanings, and use the information in the book only to help add dimension to your own ideas. Don't let it replace or change the whispers. When you pause and listen, you can access the voice within you, and you will discover your soul has much to share with you about your life.

I don't use my oracle cards to predict futures or tell fortunes. The future is fluid and always changing. Your thoughts, words and actions in this moment are the true indicator of the future you create for yourself. Instead of fortune-telling, use the symbols and meanings to enrich your day-to-day life. For example, when you pull a card about Truth, look for opportunities to live or speak your truth, or look for areas in your life where perhaps you're not being truthful. If the card is about indecision, look at what you're ambivalent about. How does your indecision serve you or hurt you? Are you choosing by *not* deciding? You will find that when you approach the cards from a place of openness and curiosity, you will be full of questions. It is those questions that help you create meaning.

One day recently, I drew a card about communication. After examining my life and 'mining the gems' from that card, I let it sit in my awareness throughout the day. When a client came in that afternoon, the first words out of her mouth were about the lack of communication in her marriage! Now, I know that card was about me, but I also know that because communication was at the top of my awareness, I was able to be genuine and helpful in our discussion. How is it that the cards always seem to touch on exactly the message you most need to hear in that moment? There are several very wise scientists and authors who could provide you with a discourse on quantum mechanics, the law of attraction, energy vibrations, and all that good stuff, and it would all be absolutely true.

My response is much simpler. It is because you already have the answers, and your soul knows the secrets you need to hear. It's up to you to be present and listen. Be sure you are asking questions that will open up possibilities rather than shut them down. For instance, when asking "What is my purpose in this life?" you are opening a very small window through which only tiny 'birds of wisdom' can fly. If you asked "What do I need to do to align myself more with my purpose?" you suddenly throw that window open wide and you find yourself with flocks of good information. One of the best questions to ask is "What do I need to know about _____?" and from Denise Linn, "What does my soul want me to know at this time?" You may find that asking about blockages is helpful. "What is blocking me from experiencing true financial abundance?" is a very powerful question, more so than "Will I ever be rich?" Instead of asking yes/no questions, you will find deeper meaning by asking open-ended questions. As you finish your readings, always remember to thank Spirit, or your ancestors, angels and spirit guides for being there with you, and ask them to assist you in opening the doors to your best life.

I mentioned earlier that it was during a reading with my cards about my life purpose that I felt the time was right for Soul Coaching training. During one of our soul journeys at Summerhill, I experienced a very deep and definite message

Hearing Messages from Spirit

AFFIRMATION: I am a clear channel for messages from Spirit.

*Believe! Right now your spirit guides, ancestors, and loved ones who have passed on are sending you messages, love, and healing. Have faith that you can discern these messages...
and you will.*

about my life purpose. Given that I'm a drum circle facilitator, the sound of beating drums resonates deeply with me. On that particular soul journey *I heard* drums in the accompanying music, and it was in that deep, constant rhythm that I heard the words "teach" and "heal". They reverberated through me with every beat... teach, heal, teach, heal. I say *I heard* because afterwards, some people were mystified as I explained to them the significance of the resonance of the drums. It seems they didn't hear any drums at all.

There is a moment, a very precious and powerful moment, near the end of the Soul Coaching training when you are invited to metaphorically 'pick up the cloak' and walk forward into acceptance of your role as guide for other people's soul journeys. When I walked across the deck and met Denise's eyes, I knew that if I turned to my right and crossed the threshold into the Sanctuary, it was going to be as a teacher and a healer and I could no longer sit in the space of 'not knowing', that stagnant, uninspiring, but *comfortable* space.

Remember the Success card that I received from Denise? On the card, there is a picture of a hand holding a star. My clients are like that star – allowing me to touch a little bit of magic each time they open the door to their best-lived lives. Read the cards, unlock the secrets and listen to the whispers. Repeat as often as needed for a rich and fulfilling best-lived life. I send you love and light for your journey.

Secrets and Whispers: Ten Steps
Step One:
Choose your oracle card deck. Browse online or a local book or metaphysical store for a deck that resonates with you. Look for artwork that inspires you, words that uplift you and a theme that works for you.

Step Two:
Connect with your deck. Look at the pictures and any words. Just let the images touch you and speak to you. Forget the book for now. Begin a journal and take notes on each of the cards if you wish. Describe what you see and ask yourself how it makes you feel. Does your card tell a story? What questions come up? Know that you may be very drawn to a particular card or cards, and there may be others that repel you. Mine both, for the gems.

Step Three:
Bless your cards. Hold them to your heart and infuse them with your loving energy. Ask that your guides and angels be present when reading the cards, and that the wisdom you receive be for your best and highest good.

Step Four:
Create a place of love and honor to store your cards. Decorate a special box infused with loving intent, wrap your cards in a precious cloth, keep them on your altar,

or wherever resonates with you. Crystals can be wonderful companions for your cards as they carry the energy of millennia of the earth's creative processes.

Step Five:
Prepare for a reading by creating a sacred space. This can be any space that you declare sacred for your purpose, and that allows you to work with your cards uninterrupted and undistracted. Have paper and pen nearby so you can write down your questions and insights, and revisit them as often as necessary.

Step Six:
Choose a spread for your reading. A spread is simply how you lay your cards out and what meaning you give to each card position. It can be as simple as a one card reading, or it can be a complex multi-card reading. You can intuitively choose a number of cards that work for your purpose, or follow the guidelines of a suggested spread in the guide book. Assign a meaning for each position.

Some examples:

- *Three Card Spreads*
  Past-Present-Future
  Gifts-Challenges-Possible Outcomes
  Mind-Body-Spirit
  Feeling-Knowing-Intuiting

- *Four Card Spreads*
  Spring-Summer-Autumn-Winter
  Air-Water-Fire-Earth

- *Seven Card Spreads*
  One for each Chakra
  One for each day of the Week

- *Twelve Card Spreads*
  One for each Month of the Year, plus one additional Overall card
  Astrological Signs and Houses

Step Seven:
Formulate the theme of your reading with one topic. Ask "What does my soul want me to know about this situation (relationship, job, task, move, etc.)?" Try not to have your question encompass more than one situation at a time or you may end up with confusion rather than clarification.

Step Eight:

Choose your cards. Lay them out in the spread you've chosen either face up or face down, again whatever feels right to you. Start with the first card position and ask yourself any of the following questions:

- What is going on in the picture, or what are the words?

- What colors, shapes, symbols and images am I noticing?

- What do I feel when I look at this?

- What meaning do these images, words and feelings have for me?

- How does this information relate to the meaning I've given to the card position and the theme or situation?

- What overall meaning does this card have for me right now?

- Is there anything else?

Step Nine:

When you are finished with the individual cards, look at the entire layout and search for patterns, overall feelings, themes, or any other information. How do they tie in to your situation? Is there a belief that is being challenged and requires new thinking? Is there an action you need to take? What are you taking away from this?

Step Ten:

Thank your Guides and Angels for their presence and ask that they help you apply this information to your life in an inspiring and useful way.

Bibliography

Arlenea, Willow and Cori, Jasmin Lee. *The Tarot of Transformation*. Red Wheel/Weiser, LLC, 2002.

Linn, Denise. *Soul Coaching Oracle Cards:* Hay House, 2005.

Lyn, Cher. *Mystic Art Medicine Oracle Cards – Tools for Transformation*. Mystic Art Medicine, 2010.

Pollack, Rachel. *Tarot Wisdom – Spiritual Teachings and Deeper Meanings*. Llewellyn Publications, 2008.

KAREN REGNANTE
Marblehead, MA, USA

KAREN HEALED HER body and transformed her life, overcoming corporate burnout, 8 years of Lyme disease, chronic fatigue and most recently cancer. In the process, she learned how to deeply connect with her intuition and follow Divine guidance, and now lives an amazingly healthy and abundantly joyful life.

Karen is a graduate of Denise Linn's Soul Coaching® Program, Hippocrates Health Institute, The New England School of Feng Shui and Young Living's Essential Oils Program. She has studied with the Dalai Lama and other Masters in the areas of feng shui, medical qigong and Sufism. She also graduated summa cum laude in Biology from Bowdoin College and has a Masters degree in Biology from UCLA.

This training combined with her 30+ years of achieving landmark results for top companies such as Apple Computer and KPMG Consulting and her transformative life experience provides her with a unique ability to help people see the Truth about their lives and make the shifts required to achieve vibrant health and true happiness.

Karen loves drawing on all of her background to help her clients connect to their intuition and Divine guidance and develop sound plans of action to live a more beautiful and fulfilling life. She's also passionate about helping women with health challenges, identify the underlying cause and creating paths to true healing. All in a fun and gentle atmosphere.

If you would like to work with Karen or have her speak at an event, please visit her website at www.KRegnante.com.

The Role of Soul in Healing

KAREN REGNANTE

Your Soul is whispering wisdom and beauty to you all the time.
You just need to hear this Voice, listen and take action
to have the life of your dreams.

For more than a decade, I had an extraordinary life, but it was the wrong life *for me*. I was a very successful Senior Marketing and Sales Executive working in New York City at the top of my field. My mind was ecstatic and satiated with the work I did and I knew I was making a difference by truly shifting the companies I worked for and their industries. And, my work provided me with a lifestyle of doing what I loved during my free time – international travel, sailing, skiing, hiking, windsurfing, diving, fine dining and enjoying the arts with my family and friends.

Sounds great, right? Well, amidst all this 'great life', my heart and Soul (and eventually, my body) were crying out for a different life. I was working 90 hour weeks and the time I got to spend doing the things I loved became less and less. I started getting messages, at first 'Whispers', when I was 40 years old. I was on a plane to Africa for a six week sabbatical from Apple Computer, where I had just received 'The Most Valuable Player Award' on my team, when I heard "Get out while you can! You are going to get sick! You can't keep pushing your body this way and not feeding your Soul!" I knew this message was true. I knew it somewhere deep inside me, but I kept saying back to my Soul… "Just a little more time. One more project, one more deal. Just a little more financial security. And, then I'll go."

In Africa I got really sick with what was thought to be typhoid fever and my health has never been the same. Out in the bush, I realized I had heard these Whispers before and had not listened. Out there with a 104 degree fever and violent vomiting for several days with only one of my best friends, the camp staff and no doctors for hundreds of miles, I thought I was going to die. I did not want to be medically evacuated because this *was* the trip of my dreams. We were on safari, deep in the African bush for two weeks, then traveling on to the Seychelles to scuba dive for two weeks and then to Chamonix, France to join two more best friends to ski for our remaining fortnight. I had been planning and dreaming of this trip for the last year and had worked so hard, I just could not imagine going home. So I stayed, and through sheer will I made it through the entire trip.

Even though I had barely escaped death there in the bush, and the whole notion of 'getting out' had really captured my attention, when I returned home, I went back to my same work pace. So much was expected of me, especially having won this award. I thought I would 'buy' enough time to accomplish my goals for the Company, myself and then be able to move on to the career I had always dreamed of, which was to help people heal holistically and open a healing spa. This had been my dream since I was 25 years old, but I still hadn't acted on it.

I spent the next 10 years, 'buying time with Soul' – being recruited by top firms, continuing to advance, creating landmark events for companies such as Compaq Computer and KPMG Consulting, and winning more awards. I worked with the top executives in the financial industry and their brilliant staffs and kept telling myself that this was such important work and I was making such great money, that it was OK to delay launching my healing center and marrying the man of my dreams. I continued to be top in my field and fulfill everyone's dreams but my Soul's. My outward life, what people saw, was a business executive who enjoyed the City, traveled constantly for business and lead international teams to forge new ground and open new markets.

Only my closest friends saw and knew that even though I enjoyed these things, my true joy came from my inward life… studying energy healing, nutrition and spirituality… that *this and being in nature or art, surrounding myself with amazing beauty and people I loved was what 'fed' me…* not what I spent 90% of my week doing. It was like I was leading a double life – my 'traditional life' during the week, and my 'spiritual' life on the weekends. And of course, the men I dated only saw the 'business executive' and all this entailed, so I attracted men who were not my soul mates. Even when I told them where I was going and what was in my heart, what they saw and wanted was this New York City persona. Then in August of 2000, quite suddenly, my body collapsed with a very serious case of Lyme disease. I had one of the worst cases ever seen and went to the top specialists in the country. It took forever to be diagnosed; I saw eight doctors before I could convince any of them I had Lyme. I *knew* I had it. My Soul Whispered to me that I had Lyme, even when none of the doctors agreed with me. I kept searching until I finally found a Lyme specialist who agreed. In fact, when I walked into his office, he said "I don't even have to test you… just looking at you I know you have a very bad case of it." When his tests came back, my readings for Lyme were off the charts.

For the next eight years I was seriously ill, five of those years confined in bed, not able to work, and almost died. I was on antibiotics for years, with a PIC line dosing into my heart. I went from someone with a brain that was great at strategy, analysis, data and figures, to a person who couldn't balance her checkbook or drive around the neighborhood without getting lost. The fevers, muscle pain, sleeplessness, the violent shakes and atrophy of my body and nervous system resulted in such debilitation that I could barely talk on the phone. I knew I was dying and drew up my will. I was so ill my lawyers had to come to my home for me to sign it.

During this phase of my illness, I went through several months of going in and out of the hospital and my mother insisted I move home, back to the Boston area. At that time, there weren't any good Lyme specialists in Boston. I was too weak to travel on my own to NYC and my parents were too elderly to drive me on a regular basis. Fortunately, at this point, I was really listening to the 'Whispers', which had now become 'Screams' from my Soul, and started following its guidance. It resulted in a path of treatment and emotional clearing that rescued my body and saved my life. All the doctors I had worked with up till that point had advised me not to do a serious detox… that I was too weak.

My Soul had been telling me for years to go to The Hippocrates Health Institute in Florida, which is known for its detox and raw vegan diet. I had put so much faith in my doctors at the time, I did not go. But now, up in the Boston area with my old support system gone, I forced myself to develop the courage to take action on what my inner Voice was saying. Every day, it told me to go to Hippocrates. Several months later I went, and within days, *I knew I had found my answer.* This was the turning point of my illness. After being there a month, I was healthy enough to go on vacation and have a wonderful time.

Since my forties, I've studied with amazing healers that helped me immensely. But it was not until I was faced with Lyme that I dramatically changed my life, diet, and ramped up my spiritual studies. During this time, I was formally introduced to 'Soul Work' when I studied with a wonderful spiritual mentor, Adair Heitmann, who taught a class called *Feeding Your Soul*. It led me to enroll and complete a three-year Feng Shui Certification Program. I'm not sure how I was able to do so being in such ill health, but I did. Denise Linn was one of my instructors and when she developed her Soul Coaching Certification Program, I couldn't wait to be part of it. I was to be in one of her first classes, but I was so ill it took me many years to be healthy enough to fly to California and study with her. After I went to Hippocrates, however, I was able to fly to the West Coast and took her class. Denise's Program helped me clear emotional and spiritual blocks that took my healing to the next level. I also got to see how these blocks had prevented me from leading a life that was truly, authentically me. Her training was the spiritual doorway I had been looking for and provided me with a great set of tools to work with.

I am so blessed to have healed completely from the Lyme. Traditional doctors do not believe this is possible, yet I know it to be true. The combination of my new lifestyle, diet and Soul Work allowed me to start my life again, to take my 30+ years of business experience to start my own company and move to the town and home of my dreams. I was practicing what I had learned and was leading a life much more in line with who I was… *but not totally.*

What I did not know back then, but I do now, was there were more major lessons to come. I was so happy, working again, living in a beautiful condo on the water with a 290 degree view of Marblehead Harbor and in a community of like-minded people. I had a life again, with deep connections to my family and friends. I was sailing, traveling to places of amazing beauty for fun, and life was going well. My business quickly took off and I was thrilled with how rapidly things manifested now that I had cleared these blocks.

One of my clients turned into practically a full time position and things were going great for the first year. However, during the second year, changes occurred at my client's company and my Soul Whispered rather loudly that I needed to replace them with new clients. But I had been sick on the couch for so many years and now I was living the life of my dreams. I was working and living in the same town, with no commute, (which after a 5 hour commute, five days a week when I lived in Connecticut and worked in NYC, seemed too good to be true). I so loved everything about the place where I lived, and being in this community. I just couldn't imagine how I could replace this client with another in this small, seacoast town which allowed me to maintain my newly-found lifestyle. I was afraid to leave; afraid I'd lose everything. The taste of this new life, health and happiness was so strong I couldn't let go.

So I stayed, *against Spirit's strong advice* and amazingly so, within a year, I got uterine cancer. No one, especially my doctors, could believe it. I so didn't fit the criteria of someone with this dis-ease. I was thin and healthy. Nonetheless, here I was sick again with another, life-threatening disease.

This time, much wiser, I immediately started my healing on the spiritual level – clearing the emotional trauma that had precipitated during these past two years as well as other issues I had not healed the first time, including the fear of fully listening to this Voice. I did this with the help of two amazing healers, Dr. Ibrahim Jaffe and Dr. Issac Goren, and added some the methodologies they taught me to my Soul Coaching techniques.

After another year, I parted with my client and my Soul Work continued. I now had to face all my fears of healing my cancer AND being out of work AND launching a new company based on my inward, *very private*, spiritual life. I'm not sure which of these was the most challenging to face. I healed a lot of the cancer spiritually and then also had surgery, because my Soul spoke so clearly that it was the way to go. It said: "You have so much living to do; it's time to get rid of it and move on to fully living an authentic life. You can heal the cancer spiritually, but it will take too much more time, so go for the surgery." So, to Mass General Hospital I went and had two surgeries back-to-back: a full hysterectomy and a lymph node dissection to insure the dis-ease hadn't physically spread.

The spiritual work I did to heal the cancer changed me so much. Now, I *totally* listen to Spirit. I don't do anything significant without first getting guidance from Spirit and listening and acting on *whatever* Soul tells me to do, *even if it seems ridiculous.* (I do however ask several times for confirmation before I act!) I have faith and trust that by listening, *whatever happens* is taking me in the direction I need to go, whether I can see it or not. This lesson was so huge. *To Trust. Really Trust.*

It has not been an easy journey, nor has the direction of my life been how I planned or thought it would go. But the life that Spirit has brought me has changed me into the person I've always wanted to be, and I am so grateful for everything that has happened, and for the life I have now. My joy and health continue to grow in leaps and bounds with each step I take that Spirit suggests.

I am no longer living in my beautiful condo, nor am in living in my seaside town of like-minded individuals. I had to temporarily let it all go in order to launch my new business and learn to accept it all… remaining joyful and trusting. In the moment, during some of these twists and turns, I couldn't believe what was happening, nor did it seem to make sense. But as time passes, the wisdom of these events is revealed and I can see how important it was for them to happen. I have now witnessed that when I ask Spirit for change and for my dreams to be fulfilled, I have to trust that the circumstances brought to me are for my highest good and in keeping with the life of my dreams, *as long as I stay connected.* Spirit is so much wiser than my mind about what is best for me, if I can only let go and let it happen.

It's been several months since I moved and I now clearly see how I've needed to be in a quiet place to hear my Soul's wisdom, and to have the space and time to bring my dreams of the future to fruition. That and spend-ing more quality time with my 88-year-old mother whom I love beyond words. My health is now soaring and my heart is full of joy and happiness… even as I walk the path of the Unknown creating my new business and learning to date men who see, appreciate and want me for who I truly am.

Denise Linn's Soul Coaching Program was the spiritual doorway that allowed me to open to my next level. Here are some of the truths I've learned during my amazing journey:

> ## Listening with Your Heart
>
> AFFIRMATION: *I trust the messages I receive from my heart.*
>
> *The heart knows what the mind cannot uncover. Trust the messages you receive from your heart. Angels and guides are communicating with you. In sweet, soft stillness, listen to their gentle whispers.*

1. All dis-ease begins on the spiritual level

Our bodies consist of many layers of energy, going from the most refined 'spiri-tual' energy to dense physical energy (i.e. the body). Emotional and spiritual trauma can be easily cleared when it's at these energetic levels, which is why it's so important to learn to discern, listen and act upon our Soul's Whispers when we hear them. So much body trauma and heartache can be avoided if we take the time to honor ourselves in this way. When dis-ease is not healed at the energetic stage, it progresses deeper into the layers of the body and finally manifests as a physical disease, something that can be identified in our body's physical form. It is not until the physical stage that Western Medicine can identify and treat the disease – *which in many cases is too late*. I'd like to share a story with you that so exemplifies this truth.

One day I was having lunch with one of my 'healthy' best friends who was leaving the next day to go to Europe for a month. As we were leaving the restaurant, she casually mentioned she had been feeling a mild, annoying pain in her side for the last few days. I convinced her to immediately go to the emergency room since she was going on this extended trip. That afternoon she was diagnosed with Stage IV ovarian cancer and passed 7 months later. She had been receiving checkups regularly and no one picked up the cancer until she had this physical symptom; no one detected it before it rapidly spread through her body. For years, however, she had been ignoring her Soul's Whispers, telling her to make a drastic change in her life… one she was not willing to make, though the consequences would be severe if she avoided the *call* to change.

Fortunately, I heard 'the call' and acted on it before it was too late. So, I ask… why go through all this hardship if instead of illness, we can be healthy and living the life of our dreams today, *right now?*

2. Our Soul talks to us at first in Whispers.
In the beginning, the Whispers can be so subtle it can almost feel like you're imagining it. For me, it began like a wisp of a few words… something so transient… it didn't seem real. As time progresses, the Whispers become a Voice. If we act at this point, it becomes a lovely, incredibly useful conversation. After that, Spirit will increase the frequency and loudness of the Voice and then do *whatever it takes* (in my case, 'screams', severe illness and almost death) to get our attention.

Our Soul is the connection point to Spirit, and Spirit is God or whatever energy we believe in. Spirit is the universal energy that connects us all and underlies all religions. It is the source of the Voice we 'hear' through our Soul. Oh how I wish I had listened to this Voice when it was at the Whisper stage!

3. All dis-ease ends on the spiritual level.
To live the life of our dreams, it is essential to find the root cause of a disease and heal it.

Even when we are fortunate enough to heal dis-ease on the physical level, we still need to clear it at the Soul level to prevent the dis-ease from reappearing or manifesting in a different way in our body or our life. I know this may be a difficult concept to embrace, but I found that when I looked at my life, I saw 'patterns' occurring over and over again. I found that underneath it all, my illnesses and even unrelated incidents were all being driven by underlying beliefs I had about myself, my life or the world. I had to identify, face and resolve major conflicts I had in my life, shift these beliefs and clear the negative emotions in my heart in order to heal. Once I identified and shifted the root cause, my life changed and my health and happiness soared.

4. Find your beauty, enjoy the day and be in LOVE no matter what is happening. Each day it is important to focus on what is wonderful in our lives and in our healing, even if it's seems to be only a small 'sliver' of our lives. *Stay with the Light, no matter what happens.* Whatever we focus on will increase, so by focusing on whatever is fabulous and healthy in our lives, we create more of it. I got through these experiences by going to bed and waking up every day *with gratitude for whatever in that day or moment was great.* I filled my body and heart with this feeling of lusciousness, regardless of the amount of physical pain I was in or procedures I was about to endure.

Some of the best times I've ever had with one of my best friends were on days I had doctors' appointments or surgery. She and I created these days as 'special outings', and as much as possible had a ball. We downplayed the fact that my body was going to be unbelievably violated with machines and chemicals, and focused on the joy we had being together, the beauty we saw, and funny things we thought of as we drove to these appointments. We were authentic in our joy and happiness because *we created the day from this point of view.* It worked because we were able to authentically create being happy. We stayed present to what was happening in *that* moment.

For example, even though I was to undergo surgery at 10 am, at 7 am, I wasn't in surgery. I was in the car with one of my best friends and we were driving along the ocean on the way to the hospital in Boston. We focused on *that*, not the surgery, which wasn't occurring for another 3 hours. I filled myself with gratitude to be with such a beautiful friend who could create this experience with me. My gratitude replaced my fear for all those moments. Even the times when I felt the fear and cried my eyes out, afterwards I would look for something to celebrate, something to be happy about or to look forward to. I tried to reduce the amount of time being frightened or upset, to *moments*, so that once the moment passed, I could return to being in joy, grace and peace.

Finding our beauty is all about getting in touch with what is authentic and real in our lives, and living from this point of view. Beauty starts on the inside, deep in our Soul, and connects us with the grace that lies within and comes from Spirit. By bringing this grace into our lives and everything we do, our lives become about 'who we are' and not our 'circumstances' or the way things 'look'. By connecting to the LOVE that is deep in our hearts, and by being this LOVE whenever possible, our lives can be transformed. *It is the LOVE that melts resistance and negative emotions, protects us, and creates positive outcomes and miracles, regardless of our circumstances.*

5. The outcome of our lives and how quickly we heal when confronted with dis-ease depends on how connected we stay to Spirit, and how much we listen and act in a timely way to the messages from our Soul.

When the fear or pain came, I found it so much easier to give in to it. But when I did, I'd notice shortly thereafter that I was no longer connected to Spirit. It is this fear and pain and choosing *'it' rather than the Light* that 'disconnects' us and brings us into darkness. Over time I learned that when I stayed connected to Spirit, and didn't go into the darkness, there was a vital message for me to hear. When I allowed Spirit to show me the message and I then acted on it, the lessons I learned were truly powerful and moved my life forward in leaps and bounds.

It's essential not to become swayed by the collective consciousness about any disease or situation in our lives. If we want to have an extraordinary, healthy life, we have to find the courage to forge our own path and listen to our own Wisdom, regardless of what others we hold dear may advise us, including our family, best friends and doctors.

It's important to listen to experts and people with vast experience or intuition. But we can spend our lives and a fortune going to 'experts' for guidance, and relying on people who really aren't an expert on the particular topic we need advice on. Each of us knows our Own Truth, and ultimately what is best for us. This includes which 'experts' to truly seek, and which advice to follow. *Only when our Soul is telling us this is Our Truth, too, does the advice makes sense to follow.*

This Truth lies deep in our heart and our Soul, and with the right tools and training, *anyone* can learn to quiet their mind, and hear these Whispers. Your Soul is whispering wisdom and beauty to you all the time. You just need to hear this Voice, listen and take action to have the life of your dreams.

◇

Opening to Love

AFFIRMATION: My heart is open.

Love is on its way. The more you open to love, the more its sweet nectar can surge through your soul. From the love of others, to the love of self, to love from the Creator, love flows to and through you. You are indeed a sacred vessel for love to flow through.

LINNEA JEWETT
Boulder, Colorado, USA

LINNEA'S LOVE FOR this wonderful world we call Earth has always been her guiding force. Her childhood near the powerful Pacific Ocean, along with her early-adult experience in the ancient Arizona Sonoran Desert inspired her to keep her mystical gateways alive. Driven by her passion to better the relationship between people and their environment, she earned a B.S. in Geography from Northern Arizona University with an emphasis in the concept of "Sense of Place". She later gave up her career as a civilian Environmentalist with the U.S Navy to stay at home with her children, hoping to provide a supportive setting for her family full of love and laughter.

As Linnea's children grew and her home became a safe exploration into the creation of sacred space, she followed her heart and studied Feng Shui at The Center for Feng Shui and Intuitive Arts in New Hampshire. After she practiced Feng Shui for a few years she realized there was more to one's immediate environment than just the placement of things and the quest for good Chi. She wanted to help people connect with not just their space, but to their souls. She was destined to find Denise Linn and became a Certified Soul Coach. Her work with Denise confirmed her spiritual notions that life is magical and magnificent.

Now in Boulder, Colorado, Linnea continues to help others find beauty in life, peace in chaos, and simply more smiles per day. For more information, please visit www.linneajewett.com

Everyday Magic in a Busy World

LINNEA JEWETT

*By making a conscious effort to remain present and focused
on the little things that delight us, we can turn down the stress
and become the sacred observer of our lives.*

It was one of those mornings when I had so much on my list of things to do. Determined to run my life like a well-oiled machine, I found myself marching up the hill to school to drop off my son by 8:20 a.m. and then rushing back home again, eager to start checking off my to-do-list. With my cell phone in hand and a headful of competing thoughts, I was aware that my daughter was walking behind me, but my mind was preoccupied. My daughter's request "Mommy" was brushed off with a quick "Yeah," while I kept walking. This distant call for my attention did not register and my focused pace never slowed. Again she said, "Mommy," this time a little louder. Her third and final attempt "MOMMY!!!" was now very loud and clear.

Not only did I hear the loud call of my daughter, but in that moment, I also then heard the loud call of my spirit. Sometimes, when I'm not paying attention, my inner whispers will turn into a booming shout. My higher self cried out, "STOP... Stop what you are doing. Don't get frustrated that she is slowing you down; stop and LISTEN!" I knew I had a choice to make. I could lecture my daughter and tell her that we had places to be and that she needed to keep up, which would have sounded something like, "Yes honey, that is a sunflower, it is pretty, BUT we have to go because we have things to do." If I had chosen that path, and there have been many times when I have, I would have missed out on the magic that was all around me, too busy to see it.

She was standing there, her little three-year-old body just the same height as the sunflower she was looking at. Honestly, I don't know who had the bigger head. There she was, nose to seed, looking at it as if she had discovered a whole new world. And that is exactly what she had done. She had opened a door to a magical realm that most of us are unaware of. Suddenly, as I took a moment, a time-out from my itinerary, I was standing in the presence of something greater than myself and my objectives. I bent down to share in my daughter's wonder to find a tiny bee with the wings of a humming bird, buzzing around little specks of pollen and seed.

The little tiny wings were beating so fast that it made the shape of an infinity sign in one consecutive motion that undulated out from its body. That's when these little wings started to sparkle with a golden brilliance and the next thing I knew, everything around me was radiant in what looked like fairy dust the color of honey. The seeds, the petals, my daughter's eyelashes, her hair blowing in the breeze, the lint on her sweater, even the iris in her eye, all glistened. I looked up and found my whole world brighter than it was before, sparkling in a golden gleam. Here I thought my daughter was given to me to help guide her throughout her life, but she had actually turned into my guide, reminding me of what was real. It wasn't just about taking time to be with my daughter, but to stop and actually see the world through her eyes. Her sweet, innocent and pure connection to the creator allowed her to show me the simple magnificence of a morning. She had become my everyday angel.

> *The divine could erupt anywhere – Earth is so thick with divine possibility that it is a wonder we can walk anywhere without cracking our shins on altars.*

—BARBARA TAYLOR

These awe-inspiring moments are everywhere just waiting for us to recognize the basic truth that life is a magical and joyful existence. Just as Barbara Taylor explained, these moments are like little altars that deserve our heartfelt reverence and appreciation. When we take the time to acknowledge these little miracles in our world, we become connected to source, spirit, and the bounty of life. This connection is what makes the difference between just going through the motions, or truly living life with an amazing amount of grace. This connection is what makes the difference between either a stressed life or joyful life. It is extremely important to connect to your blessings, the water that runs out of your faucet, the light that turns on with just a flip of a switch, the pillow that supports your head while you sleep, the song of a bird, the journey of a cloud, even the sun that rises with each new day. This new-found gratitude came rushing into me that morning with my daughter. I just needed to slow down to recognize it.

I watched the sun rise above the horizon, radiating its warm love onto our simple life below. It was as if the rays of the sun had a message for me, a message infused with light and love. That's when I knew I had to slow down and pay more attention to the details, basically everything I had been taking for granted throughout most of my life. I now looked up with a more open heart, more aware of our cosmic connectivity. As I was paying homage to our sun for its life-giving energy, something in me shifted. It took only a minute, but it felt as though time had stood still, a brief blur of infinity, much like the wings of the bee in front of us. It wasn't just the sun and this tiny bee I was linked to, but to the vibration of life all around me. I had become a sacred observer of the divine. I was in the presence of God, Goddess, the creator, our source, true light and love. It was more than just noticing the beauty of nature; it was a moment that infused itself into every cell of my body. It was as if the divine essence of the sunflower seed planted itself in me and now I had this seed of understanding, patiently waiting to grow with each new future experience. Life was never the same again.

It wasn't long after the incident with my daughter and the sunflower that I found myself enrolled in Denise Linn's Soul Coaching course. I took my new way of viewing the world into my work with Denise, as it supported and heightened how I wanted to practice my personal and professional life. I wanted to be of service to my family, my friends, and my clients, helping them to find that same level of magnificence in their life. It is my goal to raise the level of joy in our world, particularly since people seem to be experiencing so much stress these days.

It is this stress and our hectic way of living that can disconnect us from our spirit, keeping us from finding true contentment and playful magic. How many times have we said to ourselves we 'should' or 'shouldn't' have done this or that? How many times have we rushed from one task to another, never taking a good look at the beauty that abounds around us? It is as if our ego places blinders on us, only allowing us to focus on the source of our stress. We cling to this stress because in some sort of dysfunctional way our ego tells us that we are doing something right. We must be doing something right if we are fixated on fixing the problem, and we think our happiness will begin once these problems are solved. Whatever our current roles are, parent, spouse, son, daughter, neighbor, homeowner, employer, or employee, of course we want to be the best at what we set out to do. And sure, a little pressure from stress can get the job done, but just remember too much stress can blind us. It can preoccupy our every moment, so that we are no longer aware of the great pleasure simple delights can bring. It is actually these simple delights that help manage the stress, but we first must connect to them.

For me, I needed to challenge the idea that I could still find these gifts of magic in my crazy active world, which, as a full time Mom is filled with so many unwanted distractions and self-made stresses. This was put to the test when I was required to take a Vision Quest in Nature after my course work with Denise. I whole-heartedly appreciate why a vision quest is best experienced in a place of nature; nature gives us an opportunity to pause and stimulates our awareness of source and creation. Our physical bodies feel at home with all the elements and our spirit bodies are given room to soar. Many signs and teachings can come to us from this realm just outside our door. However, I'm like so many other people who are unable to run into the woods at the drop of a hat when they feel so inclined. So, I decided to have the same kind of experience I had with my daughter in front of the sunflower, in the middle of a bustling city.

I made the choice to take my vision quest to the urban jungle of Denver. I needed to know that no matter where we are or how chaotic or stressful our surroundings may be, we can still hear the inner whispers of our higher self. We can still find bits of sparkle. To do this involves taking pause, being connected in the moment and finding the pleasure of life in the smallest of detail.

I allowed my spirit to guide me through the concrete maze of sidewalks and buildings. I could have allowed the buzz of an active city to distract me and fluster me into thinking this was a bad idea, but I stayed true to my search. I soon found a bench made of reclaimed wood from Indonesia. It just happened to be sitting out in front of a store for sale. My soul whispered "Sit", and so I did. I asked myself how many people must have walked passed this little offering of solitude, not even aware of its contribution. The wood was twisted together to make a work of art, and as I sat down, I could feel the rootedness of the wood.

The bench soothed my soul. The warm energy of the wood slowed me down and I had once again become a sacred observer to the world around me. With my face turned to the sun, I noticed the air, the slight breeze blowing across my skin, the sounds of sparrows that could now be heard over the roar of cars rushing past, and the people walking by. I thought to myself, would the people passing by take any notice of me? Here I was, a woman, shoulders relaxed with a big smile on my face as I soaked in the sunlight. Again the message of connection whispered in my soul. Did my smile put a smile on their face? In that split instant, did they feel more at peace just by witnessing my sense of peace, or did their daily stresses dull their senses so that their blinders blocked out any ripples of possible connection. When we take those blinders off and start observing from the heart, we will discover that the vibration of joy, happiness, and the smiles from others can grow into something highly contagious.

While I was working on this chapter, I had the privilege to experience this type of connection I am referring to. I was sitting in my local café, when my soul whispered "Look up". There she was, a woman seated four tables down, and just in that moment her food was placed in front of her. She gracefully placed her hands together and lowered her head. I watched her pray, and though I don't know what she said, I could see her lips move with purpose and intention. I have seen people pray before meals as if they were checking off a box on their spiritual to-do-list, but I had never witnessed such a heart connection put into a prayer like this before. I could actually feel ripples of appreciation and love flow out of her and through me as this amazing energy was then released out into the universe.

Savoring Pleasure

AFFIRMATION: I fully embrace bliss in my life.

Fill your life with people, experiences, and places that bring you delight and joy. Live deliciously! Release the need to be practical in all situations. Surround yourself with beauty and sumptuous pleasures.

I instantly became more light-hearted and less stressed about the judgments I was currently placing on myself concerning my writing skills.

This moment was so brief, but so significant that I had to share with her the gift she gave me before she left. I told her how honored I was to have felt her love and was transformed by her prayer. Tears filled her eyes as she asked "You felt that?" I answered "Yes". She then began to tell me that she was faced with a lot of uncertainty and hard times, but that she didn't want to complain. She explained that she had so much appreciation for the little things, such as a good meal or a chance encounter with a stranger. She wanted to focus on her blessings rather than her stresses. Before leaving the café, she gave me a big hug, telling me that I had made her day; when in actuality she had made mine and I will never forget her.

When we become present in our current moment, our souls have the capability to seek out blessings in the face of obstacles. This is a conscious effort to remain focused and grateful for the things that support and replenish us. Bringing our attention to what is positive teaches us that life can be a wonderful experience. We will find peace in our chaos and fluidity from one event to another. We are allowed to ride a wave of pain with much more grace. We can take a deep breath, relax our shoulders and find an unconditional quality in 'what is'. This does not mean that we sign ourselves up for complacency and abuse. What it does mean is that by staying connected to the ongoing search for beauty and magic, our path in life will be based on the truth of our soul. We do not want to judge what this path may look like.

Self-judgment will only muddle the development of our sacred relationship with self and the world we live in. Judgment comes from a place of right and wrong, and when we judge, we integrate heaviness into our emotional body. I know this because as a mother, judgment has a way of creeping in. It has kept me on a strict schedule; it has made me envious of others; it has contributed to huge amounts of guilt, and has burdened me with perfectionism. To this day, I still fight the tendency to want to judge myself and critique my efforts. The irony of my judgment is that the critic that resides in me thinks she knows everything, always telling the other more insecure parts of myself that I don't know enough. How funny that these are two different parts of me residing in the same body. It seems almost comical.

There's a wonderful Taoist story that I've been reading to my children for many years. *The Farmer's Luck* is a great example of how to live without judgment. The farmer finds himself in many different life-changing situations that most of us would categorize as either good or bad. His neighbors always come around to express their evaluation of what has just happened, "Oh, what a shame. Such bad luck." But without bias, the farmer merely replies, "Hmm, we shall see." This farmer is the perfect model of a sacred observer. He does not put too much emphasis on what may appear to be bad or good. He just flows from one moment to the next, knowing the whole story is yet to be seen. You may have heard the clichés 'You never know' and 'Things aren't always as they appear'. Well, I am here to remind you that there is great truth in these simple words.

My husband had the fortunate opportunity to work in Taiwan in his younger years, quite a life changing experience for him. I love the stories he shares with me about living abroad, but this one is my favorite. One very late and fateful night, he found himself stuck working in the lab, trying to finish a project before boarding a flight over to a neighboring island. As he continued to work, he became quite frustrated and anxious about how late it was getting, well into the wee hours of morning. In those early hours of that morning, he decided that he was too exhausted to fly, and with great disappointment, he cancelled his trip that day. He was broken-hearted about this decision because the island he was going to visit was a highly sought-out destination for tourists, renowned for its beauty. This flight that he was not meant to travel on was never found again. Lost at sea, the plane's door was the only thing they ever recovered. As the tale of *The Farmer's Luck* suggests, we don't know the whole story.

We often give so much power to our stories; either the story of our past, or the story yet to be seen. At times we can get lost in it, stuck in a state of judgment or fear. We can lose sight of the fact that these judgments and fears can and will shape the way we perceive ourselves, others, and our experiences. I remember Denise Linn saying, "We are not our events; it is the meanings we give to these events that is significant." The storyline and dialog we are conducting in our head can proclaim good, loving, strong opinions of self, or negative, self-destructing ones. The emotions you attach to an event can become like a broken record, playing over and over in your head, proclaiming to the world "This is who I AM; these are my circumstances and there is nothing I can do to change that." Your story can become a stuck identity.

Ten years ago I became a mother, a very significant event that created a new identity for me. Yet I wasted too many precious moments in the beginning because I was attached to the bitterness of the selflessness of parenting, the lack of sleep, the lack of showers, the long days spent separated from the bustle of the world, not to mention that the housework seemed to have quadrupled. The bitter meaning I gave my circumstance, which was born out of frustration, kept me from enjoying it fully. Though motherhood was often a stressful task, as I got the hang of it, I felt a stirring within me. That stirring was a desire to create sacredness in my life, to change the meaning I had shaped in my mind about staying at home with my children. The more I became aware of my thoughts and my surroundings, the more open I became to how fulfilling motherhood could be. Through time, I transformed into a spiritual homemaker rather than 'just an at-home-mom'.

I know that the fast pace of this post-industrial world can become so over whelming and exhausting that it can stunt our natural sense of playfulness and exploration. We get physically drained from keeping up in this wild race our culture has placed us in. Sometimes it is all we can do to just breathe, but when we are running from one task to another without awareness and openness, we can overlook opportunities and possibilities. Much like I could have overlooked the joy of a simple morning. Don't miss the sparkle, the blessings, and your connection with yourself and with others. Remember not to rush through life, but rather to be in awe of it, like the sacred observer.

If we can become the sacred observer, we can honor where we are in our own process, even if the moment doesn't feel so good. It is natural that emotional feelings will surface as we experience life, but as the sacred observer, we can find comfort in knowing these feelings will not last. We can honor the phase, the energy level, the cycle we are currently in. Just like the river, it is always flowing, moving, and impermanent. Just as my children are moving through development, so too are we. Just as they learned to walk, so are we taking steps towards our dreams. Sometimes they are only baby steps and sometimes they are great big giant leaps. Whatever this winding path through life may feel like to you, if you just observe it without judgment, you will be free to walk, dance, skip, or stroll to your heart's content.

I share my stories with you not because I have the secret to a great mystery, or that my solution has been researched and studied for many years and bears the weight of scientific proof. I share my stories in hopes that you are inspired, reminded, and validated in what you already know, just how simple joy can be. Life in our modern world moves fast, and as we learn to be super-efficient with our time, we can also rob ourselves of a little bit of magic that could go a long way. It is important to have goals, dreams, and ambitions, but when we stubbornly insist on dictating how life 'should' look, then we become inflexible, and blind to amazing possibility.

The Practice of Being a Sacred Observer

I do not claim to know anything you don't already know,
but if I can help you to remember then I am blessed.

—RABBI SHAPIRO

Before I give you some tips and techniques on becoming your own sacred observer, it is important for you to first honor yourself and notice how you are feeling in this moment. Knowing your current level of energy allows you to be accepting of your output. It is essential to not feel guilty, or judge too heavily if you do not meet your expectations. I will tell you what I tell my kids, "It's ok; don't beat yourself up, because life is about growing and learning; we didn't come here as perfect beings, knowing everything, so let's make a promise to be perfectly imperfect." Then I would make a little joke, find some humor and ask them to try again. Remember, humor is a great resource when trying to manage self-judgments. Laughing at ourselves is a wonderful cure for lifting our vibration.

By choosing to become a sacred observer, you are making a promise to yourself to be without judgment. So what if you didn't take your vitamins or that the laundry is still in a pile on the floor! Yes, these are simple examples that have a minimal impact on our life, but you can apply this philosophy to even bigger situations. Releasing ourselves of judgment and attachment can be difficult because they are so heavily engrained in our way of being. So, just as I would request my children to be kind with themselves as they grow, I request the same of you. Grant yourself the permission to not be perfect.

Once you have released yourself from perfectionism, you can begin each day with an open heart. I suggest that in these next few days, you start to awaken your senses to the world around you. Give yourself permission to slow down so that you do not miss divine opportunity. Our Creator made this world to be enjoyed with everything we have. There is an abundance of magical treasures to delight in, as big as the night sky and the vast universe or as small as pollen on a sunflower seed. Watch, touch, smell, listen and breathe. Be open to unexpected ways of experiencing happiness. Be that person who stops to smell a rose in public or initiates an exchange of smiles with a stranger. Call an old friend or take a bath in solitude. Whatever that moment of magic looks like for you, seek it out! Soak it in, love it, rub up against it, and breathe it into every cell of your body, because it is these moments that will raise your level of vibration.

Once you have become playfully connected to your senses and have transformed into a seeker of joy, you will have the ability to experience mini vision quests on a daily basis. I use the term 'vision quest' in the sense that you are allowing and observing your mystical connection to the everyday happenings around you. As Denise Linn suggests in her *Soul Coaching* book, "Watch for signs, coincidences, and synchronicities. Ask yourself the following about every experience today: *If this event had a message for my life, what would it be?*" Open yourself up and notice the magic all around you. Taking the time to witness and watch for signs will give you a greater sense of clarity; which in return will allow you to become more empowered with the choices you make in life.

My story represents a simple truth. When you slow down to look and listen, you will find that you are a sacred observer, that you can hear the whispers of your soul. Remember to be motivated from your heart. Be patient with yourself, and don't forget to play!

∽

Bibliography
Taylor, Barbara. *An Altar in the World: A Geography of Faith.* HarperCollins, 2009.
Linn, Denise. *Soul Coaching.* Hay House, 2003.
Shapiro, Rabbi Rami. "Is It Important To Find a Good Spiritual Teacher?" in *Spirituality & Health*, Issue: March-April, 2011.

Soaring into Joy

AFFIRMATION: Childlike wonder fills my life.

Celebrate and live life with glee!
Clap your hands in delight!
Be madcap and spontaneous!
All is truly well.

VICTORIA COEN
Seattle, Washington, USA

GUIDED BY HER insatiable curiosity, quest for deeper meaning, empathetic heart and keen intuition, Victoria Coen has chosen a diverse career path, bridging the practices of Psychology, Spirituality, Energy Healing and Feng Shui. Her passion and expertise for creating inner harmony in the lives and homes of her clients has been sought out in television and radio interviews as well as numerous magazine and newspaper publications for the past three decades.

As an international speaker, university instructor and collaborator with a world-wide team of writers for a humanitarian movie called "The Difference", Victoria is on a perpetual mission to encourage the expansion of her own and others' higher consciousness. Toward this end, she received a Master's degree in Social Work and brings her nurturing and compassionate nature to her successful psychotherapy private practice of 31 years. By empowering her clients to access their own inner wisdom, Victoria delights in this co-creative healing process which transforms their lives, infusing them with greater passion, purpose and peace.

On her continuing quest to enlighten, inspire and elevate her spirit and that of others, Victoria has also become a Certified Feng Shui Consultant, Certified Soul Coach, Transformational Energy Healer, avid meditator, traveler, gardener, animal lover and published poet.

While residing in Seattle, Washington, Victoria embraces the beauty of nature surrounding her as well as the frequent opportunities to practice gratitude when it rains nearly 8 months of the year! To contact Victoria, visit her website at www.VictoriaCoen.com

The Courage to Choose Gratitude – No Matter What

VICTORIA COEN

To speak gratitude is courteous and pleasant, to enact gratitude is generous and noble, but to live gratitude is to touch Heaven.

—JOHANNES GAERTNER

As we sat across from each other, cross-legged on the ground, I was in awe of his immensely peaceful presence. Ensconced in a magnificent feather headdress and well-worn supple leather clothing, it was evident he was a Native American Chief, a keeper of the Sacred Wisdom. He looked at me with his deeply penetrating gaze and soulful knowing eyes, and I knew he had an important message for me.

I was brought to this Native American elder by a black lab dog named Molly, who led me deliberately through a field of tall flaxen grass with a subtle urgency in her stride. When we arrived at an old, seemingly abandoned cabin in the woods, Molly sat down outside the door. As the cabin door opened, rusty hinges creaking as it widened, I stepped inside to see the Chief sitting quietly on a blanket as if expecting me. With his gentle smile and long grey braids, he invited me to sit down directly in front of him. He called himself 'Grandfather Moon'. Looking at him with great anticipation, I waited for his message.

He said "You have all you need. Use it. Let people in to help you. They are all around you. They are always there. You are not alone." Then Grandfather Moon ceremoniously picked up his carved wooden pipe, took a puff and shared it with me, simply saying "Be well." I was mesmerized by his radiant skin, the kindness emanating from his wise face and the peace I felt in his luminous aura. Although wishing to linger, I sensed his message was complete. So I stood up, thanked him graciously and left the cabin. Molly-dog was still sitting patiently outside the door, waiting to escort me back through the vast open field. We walked side by side, Molly with her usual exuberant gait and me with renewed assurance that I was not alone. I clearly knew that Grandfather Moon was among my many seen and unseen 'helpers' who were waiting in the wings to assist me on my life's path. *Then I opened my eyes.*

After this guided meditation ended, I brought my awareness back into the present moment where I was sitting comfortably on a beautiful patio in the radiant sun. This concluded my first Soul Journey. The amazing experience took place at my Soul Coaching Professional Certification training with founder Denise Linn, at her sublime Summerhill Ranch in California.

I entered my Soul Journey with the question "How can I do better self-care?" What I came away with, thanks to the wisdom of Grandfather Moon, was that I am continually surrounded by love and support. In fact, he strongly emphasized that my self-care doesn't need to be a solo endeavor but rather a joint venture of seeking others' assistance. Whether coupled or single, this has *not* been easy for me as I have been primarily on 'independent auto pilot' all my life. Content in the driver's seat, I've been humming down the road of life (favoring the fast lane!) with frequent success. Ask for help? Who me? That would be quite unusual for this self-sufficient gal. But who am I to question the sage advice of my Native American teacher?

Soul Journeys are a vital component of Soul Coaching, the sacred practice of discovering our authentic self and creating a meaningful life in complete alignment with it. During my guided sojourn, relaxing words calmed my body, allowing me to "sink deep beneath everyday life into the realm of inner truth." Denise Linn further reveals: "There is a special place within you that knows exactly what your soul needs. These relaxation techniques allow you to tap into that sacred inner wisdom to discover your own answers."

Continuing on with my Soul Journey, I found myself in a nature setting requesting to meet my Soul Messenger, who may come in any form, whether human, non-human, animal, Spirit Guide, Angel, etc. In this case, Grandfather Moon appeared as my Soul Messenger. I asked him for advice pertaining to my initial question or anything vital for me to know at that time. Once Grandfather Moon shared his message, I intuitively knew that I could re-visit him anytime in the future. At that moment, I couldn't begin to imagine his significance in my life ahead.

Another one of my Soul Journeys began with the question: "Should I buy a house?" That guided voyage led me to a home that I was not especially fond of, but could see its 'diamond in the rough' potential. My Soul Messenger was a jovial emerald frog who appeared at the end, advising me to "Buy it, Buy it!" I wondered if I heard correctly as this was *not* my long-imagined dream home. Yet, as musician Mick Jagger has reminded us, we don't always get what we *want*, but we do get what we *need*.

The world will give you the exact experiences you need
for the evolution of your consciousness.

—ECKHART TOLLE

Historically, my real-life house hunting expedition began in 1987 during one of Seattle real estate's great buying frenzies. As a novice, I jumped into this wild world with eager anticipation and came out with *no* home and $2,500 *less* in my bank account! Needless to say, my initial foray into house buying was devastating. However, I couldn't resist the lure of a seductively beckoning Open House sign on countless Sunday afternoons, keeping alive my optimism for eventual home ownership.

Fortified with renewed hope and encouraged by the remarkably low interest rate, I bravely plunged into the housing market again in 2010. After a year dedicated to searching almost every weekend, I found a home that I loved and felt inexplicably happy in when visiting there with my realtor. Bizarrely, the owners suddenly took it off the market before considering my offer.

Dejected but not deterred, while doing another exhaustive online housing search, I came upon a listing that was *not* in my preferred neighborhood. Typically, I would delete such homes. But for some mysterious reason, I pursued this listing and noted its prime location across the street from a park. With moderate enthusiasm, I viewed the home and was actually quite impressed. Through a series of very unusual and truly synchronistic events, I successfully purchased this home two months later, even though a competing foreign investor offered the Seller a sizable sum *above* the asking price and *all cash*!

After telling friends that I purchased this home, I walked around my old neighborhood, adoring the vintage architecture, and feeling quite apprehensive about my pending move. Strolling down the sidewalk, I suddenly saw the clear image of Grandfather Moon standing just ahead of me, smiling silently and nodding his head in approval of my decision. This powerful and unexpected affirmation caught me by surprise but I was very grateful for his reassurance at such a pivotal moment.

After two months of seemingly endless packing and purging, I moved into my new house. It's a lovely modern three-story home with a compelling park view but with surprisingly little vintage Craftsman charm I had longed for since being a teenager, with my nose buried in home design magazines. So why did I buy this home? Where did my dream of the quintessentially quaint, classic cottage go? Apparently, out my new third story window!

And then the 'fun' began.

On the evening of moving day, after the movers and my friends had gone home, I sat staring at the blank walls in utter disbelief. How had I landed *here*? And why? The mystery and the *misery* began to unfold. For the entire month to follow, I intensely loathed being in my new house. I refused to unpack any boxes except the bare necessities since I did *not* want to be there. As I went to work each morning, I felt immediate relief when leaving my house and reveled in the oasis of my comfortable office where I loved being with my psychotherapy clients.

Upon returning home at night, an overwhelming sense of debilitating dread came over me, like the darkest of black clouds looming oppressively overhead. This shrouded me with intense despair and paralyzing inertia, as if I were cloaked in an invisible lead straight jacket. Who had pulled my energetic plug? All I could do was sit on my couch and stare stoically into space until bedtime when I sought refuge in sleep.

Uncannily, my television, phone and internet were all unavailable that entire first month since the companies delivering these services made numerous errors while attempting to connect my service. Even my beloved books remained packed in tall towers of boxes that overwhelmingly surrounded me. Beyond tired, bone-achingly exhausted, my reserve tank was empty. For a person who always fervently believes that there are no accidents and who considers herself 'an incurable optimist' with her glass ¾ full, my astonishing state of emotional and physical distress was very foreign territory.

Within two days of moving in, I came home after running errands to find my sweet dog mysteriously injured and in shock. Frantically, I called a dear friend to drive us to the Emergency Veterinary Hospital, and after two hours of tests and X-rays, his back injury was diagnosed and treated. The next day when I returned home, the smoke alarm was loudly screeching *only* in the room my dog was staying in! Mysteriously, there was *no* fire. He was sadly traumatized again. The following morning, upon leaving for work, my automatic garage door wouldn't open, trapping my car inside. Two hours later the garage repair company arrived, pushed the garage door opener button and it immediately worked perfectly! What invisible trickster was inhabiting my new abode? Was I being taunted by unseen forces, and if so, it would apparently take more than me alone to dispel them and revive both my inner resources and my surroundings.

Expecting Miracles

AFFIRMATION: Miracles are blossoming in my life.

Majestic wonders are unfolding for you, even as you read this. Watch for them and embrace them. The more you become aware of the small marvels in your life, the more they will grow in magnitude around you.

Undoubtedly sensing their presence, my dog wanted an escape route too. In my former house, he was quite content staying home alone. Here, however, after only a few days of leaving my precious pooch home alone, I returned from work one evening to find a note on my front door from an anonymous neighbor stating that my dog had been barking incessantly and "disturbing the peace." Until I could find another option, my dog came to work with me the next day, and the next...

At this point, I wondered again if I had made a colossal mistake in purchasing this house. Clearly, my predicament was much more than 'buyer's remorse'. I vacillated between "Why is this happening *to me?*" (the ever-popular Victim stance) and "Why did *I manifest* this house into my life?" (the gaining-popularity Self-Empowerment stance). How could my expertise as a Feng Shui Consultant with 16 years of experience, plus my 12 years of well-honed skills as an Energy Clearing Practitioner and my keen intuition have chosen a home that was creating such utter chaos? And how soon could I move out? The next morning, I was on the verge of calling the movers who brought me here and having them transport my belongings to a storage facility. My dog and I would stay in a hotel until I could find a place to *rent!* Instead, I did what Grandfather Moon advised me to do two years earlier… I asked for help.

Desperately seeking to shift the negative energy of this vexing place, I asked three fellow Energy Clearing Practitioners to work remotely on cleansing my house. Then, calling upon another dear friend for help, we conducted the Violet Flame Invocation together. This extremely potent meditation harnesses unsavory energy and transmutes it into pure light. From that moment on, as a result of courageously calling in my friends to purify my home, I have felt uplifted with a renewed sense of groundedness, encouragement and hope. Now my home feels more energetically unencumbered and revitalized, gradually becoming my sacred sanctuary from which to launch the life of my dreams.

Reflecting back upon my bedtime ritual every night of that miserable month, even in the midst of tremendous doubt and confusion, I somehow mustered the courage to tell my spiritual guides how grateful I was to be a home owner and ask for their help in deciphering why I was here. Knowing full well there was a reason this house was meant for me, I politely requested that they *please enlighten me at their earliest convenience!* I welcomed these brief moments of peace and solace when expressing my gratitude to them, while reminding myself of the bigger picture still unfolding in this divinely guided plan.

The seemingly simple yet courageous act of surrendering and asking for help profoundly transformed my life. Through recognizing the ironic strength and boldness involved in being vulnerable and dependent on others, I can now view asking for help as a *healthy* dependency. This leads to *interdependence*, reflecting a mutual reliance or reciprocal exchange between people where equanimity exists. The deeper connection I feel with others resulting from these rich interactions now make it truly desirable to reach out.

Additionally significant for me was realizing that if my house ordeal hadn't been so immobilizing, I surely would have attempted to handle it alone and foolishly shunned my lesson of asking for support. After all, I had previously dealt with cancer and a debilitating car accident with only minimal requests for help. *Not so wise!* Through this current adversity, I learned how to walk the tightrope between self-sufficiency and need. Indeed, to renounce our ego's pride and invoke our soul's wisdom is a major step toward spiritual maturity.

For years in my clinical practice, I have often asked my psychotherapy clients: "What did you learn about yourself that this problem was perfect to teach you?"

I recall one client saying how grateful she was for a dear friend who read her favorite books aloud to her while in the hospital receiving chemotherapy. Through this experience, my client realized she had neglected her friends and her love of books in favor of her fast-paced lifestyle. In the midst of her courageous cancer treatment, she learned to be grateful for this precious time to deepen her friendships and to re-assess her skewed life priorities. I, too, have learned how gratitude, that magic elixir, can heal our wounds, reveal our courage, remove obstacles, and inspire the flow of abundance in our lives. And professionally, I'm thankful for the added benefit coming from my challenging home experience which is the deepening compassion I feel for my clients when they are enduring serious turmoil.

Shortly after my homecoming, two new neighbors shared with me a brief history of the park across the street. Upon further research, I discovered it had been a sacred Native American ceremonial ground and the site of natural mineral springs and sweat lodges used for medicinal healing until the mid-1800s. The mineral springs still remain, now sheltered by a tall grove of trees, offering safe haven for ducks and other wildlife. As I envision this land occupied by the original Native Americans conducting their sacred healing rituals on this auspicious site, I have profound appreciation for this holy land upon which my new home resides, and for the cultural heritage that is steeped in my new neighborhood.

Now I *finally* know why I live in this house and whose guidance led me here. Thank you, Grandfather Moon, for your encouragement to persevere – *no matter what* – because there is always a reason, a purpose and a path. I hold enormous gratitude in my heart and soul for the privilege of living on *your* land, beside *your* healing waters. With utmost reverence and respect, I will cherish this sacred space with which you have entrusted me.

Spreading our gratitude further, my dog and I are both thankful to my new neighbor who informed me of his barking while home alone. This has resulted in my dog coming to my office every day where he proudly plays the role of 'honorary therapy dog'. His spunky yet calming presence in my psychotherapy office brings spontaneous smiles to the faces of my clients and colleagues alike. As the new 'office mascot', he is truly a bundle of joy on four legs and a welcome addition to my office.

My deepest gratitude extends to Denise Linn, my extraordinary Soul Coaching teacher. With her uncompromising belief that "The Soul loves the Truth," she has graciously led me on a holy journey, further deepening my spiritual connection with myself. Denise wisely says "It is not what happens during the Soul Journey, but rather what happens in our life afterwards that really matters." The manifestation of my new home is only one in a marvelous succession of positive changes that have followed my precious time with her. She is a bountiful blessing, an infinitely gifted mentor and a profound wisdom bearer on my path to living the life of my dreams.

If the only prayer you ever say is 'Thank You', that will be enough.
—MEISTER ECKHART

Choosing gratitude – *No matter what?*

Understandably, gratitude is likely the *last* thing we feel during tumultuous times. And seeing the elusive *gift* while in the middle of a traumatic event may seem impossible to conceive. But at least consider that one exists, yet to be revealed. Most often, we go to a dark emotional place where fear, hurt, anger, sadness, grief and resentment reside. We want to shake our fist at the sky, at God, at the doctor who gave us upsetting news, at the boss who laid us off, or at our partner who chose someone else. These feelings are certainly expected during a healing crisis. So allow yourself to fully feel the experience and lean *into* it as much as possible, rather than away from it. Doing so could lead to deepening your inner self-knowledge, a new revelation or profound awakening. It may even expand your consciousness to allow your soul greater capacity to hold more light.

In neuroscience, we're told that thinking grateful thoughts can activate the part of the brain that floods our bodies with endorphins, the feel-good hormones. Cultivating gratitude can also strengthen our psychological immune system, enhancing our ability to transform crisis into opportunity. If we don't believe we are owed or entitled to blessings, nor feel punished when misfortune befalls us, then we can more easily embrace gratitude, *no matter what.*

Does the Universe act in capricious ways to bring suffering upon us just to test our resolve to be grateful? If so, this could be a valuable exercise in patience, persistence and resilience. Would you enroll in a class called "Adversity 101" to learn these lessons? Certainly not intentionally, but if life escorts you to this 'classroom', vow to emerge at the end of the semester with an evolved perspective on this paradoxical pursuit of feeling grateful even while suffering. Your ever-evolving consciousness will thank you.

Dance when you're broken open. Dance if you've torn the bandage off.
Dance in the middle of fighting. Dance when you're perfectly free.

—RUMI

Why does it take *courage* to choose gratitude?

Indeed, it takes tremendous courage to say "Thank You" while in the grip of adversity, *before* you see the light at the end of the tunnel or the silver lining revealed behind the clouds. It is relatively easy to be thankful when times are good. But the most courageous time to believe you will not be swallowed up by the tidal wave is *during* the heart-pounding escape from danger. And yet this is highly counter-intuitive. But that is part of the exquisite perfection of this courageous act of choosing gratitude at the most inopportune times.

Scientists tell us about the calm 'eye' in the center of a whirling tornado. Yes, even the natural world has organized itself with a place of refuge in the midst of chaos. So perhaps you can attempt to summon your courage and find moments of calm within you while weathering your storms. Remembering to ask for help from those who not only believe in you and your strengths, but also embody this courage themselves, can be of monumental support. After all, *you* are not alone either. Hence, gratitude is not merely an emotion we feel when reaping life's blessings, but also a courageous attitude towards life, untethered from our circumstances, both fortunate and unfortunate.

So be a student of gratitude. Let the hardship be your lesson and let courage be your teacher. Gratitude softens us and courage makes us stronger. The marriage of these two gives birth to love, hope, compassion and joy. Choose gratitude not only when fear and pain have subsided and the gifts have been revealed, but courageously choose gratitude, *no matter what*, if even for just a moment during the crisis. When allowing ourselves to be broken open by challenges rather than broken down by them, we can live from a more authentic spirit where gratitude becomes a way of life. The extraordinary reward for this daring act is opening a window to your heart which lets the light of the Divine shine in.

> *Gratitude is an inner light that can illumine our soul.*
> *The more we are thankful, the more light we experience*
> *and the more we can shine forth into the world.*
>
> —M.J. RYAN

Gratitude In Action

The expression of gratitude in our lives is derived from gradual, dedicated and conscious practice. This comes from actively engaging our mind, heart and overall awareness to recognize gratitude-inspiring opportunities, summon the courage to be thankful *during* life's storms, convey appreciation to those cherished supporters who help us, and internalize the benevolent gifts concealed in every crisis. Essentially, gratitude is a choice we could make in almost any moment, yet when mired in stressful situations we understandably become oblivious to this opportunity. But our hardship can play a vital role in birthing gratitude. Ultimately, when we transform our suffering into thankfulness, we begin manifesting a more empowered life, finding deeper meaning in our experiences. Here are some exercises to explore for cultivating more gratitude in your life and for keeping your beloved soul and spirit aloft.

Blessings in Disguise – Past and Present

Think about five past experiences in your life that you initially perceived as a curse but later discovered were blessings in disguise. Recall key people who influenced those events, and contemplate your emotions, actions and reactions involved. Write down these events along with the gifts they eventually revealed to you and what you were grateful for about those experiences. How did you transform your pain into power to resolve those problems? Were you able to experience gratitude during those crises? Now, think about a current difficulty, large or small, and courageously stretch yourself to find something about it you could choose to feel grateful for. Then read your list of five past blessings to remind yourself that your present challenge also has a hidden gift awaiting you. Trusting and believing this takes courage, but it's worth it! *Hint:* Keep your past blessings list handy and read it in the midst of turmoil when you need a positive dose of hope and encouragement.

Gratitude Meditation – The Oyster and the Pearl

This meditation is derived from a Buddhist story of profound compassion for embracing and transmuting obstacles. It focuses on envisioning the transformation of a grain of sand into the jewel of a pearl inside the oyster. Breathe gently and deeply into a state of peaceful relaxation. Imagine a tiny grain of sand being patiently embraced within an oyster, swaying back and forth in the ocean's current until a lustrous pearl is formed. Then ponder some of your life circumstances which have begun as annoying grains of sand and with love, patience and compassion have been transformed into precious jewels. Allow yourself to be grateful for the sand (your obstacles or imperfections), and the pearl (the resulting gift), as well as the surrounding oyster shell (your friends, family, spiritual guides, etc.) within which this metamorphosis occurred. Now, make a list of the pivotal people who have accepted, encouraged and loved you through your various crises. Consider writing them *hand-written* thank you notes conveying appreciation for their generous assistance.

Gratitude Potluck Celebration!

Celebrate those people who have graciously supported you on your journey, rejoicing in your wondrous spirit of resilience in overcoming obstacles. Hold a gratitude gathering and invite everyone to bring a food item to share, along with stories of thankfulness about pivotal experiences that have changed their lives, the lessons they have learned and the gifts they have gleaned from them. You as the host may wish to prepare a special gift or written message you will share with each guest to express your deep appreciation for their blessing in your life. Now celebrate the magnificence in all of you, and in your magically inspired, heart-centered, soulfully sensuous lives of abundance! The life of your dreams is ever-unfolding. Seize it, savor it and soar!

❧

Bibliography

Hay, Louise. *Gratitude, A Way of Life*. Hay House, Inc., 1996.
Lesowitz, Nina and Sammons, Mary Beth. *Living Life as a Thank You*. Cleis Press, 2009.
Ryan, M.J. *Attitudes of Gratitude*. Conari Press, 1999.
Shelton, Charles. *The Gratitude Factor*. Hidden Spring Books, 2010.
Tolle, Eckhart. *A New Earth*. Penguin Books, 2005.

Blessing

May the Spirit of Air be with you
keeping your thoughts pure
as you greet each new day,
each moment, a new beginning,
an opportunity to grow.

May the Spirit of Water be with you
balancing your emotions,
like the freshness of rain, the serenity of a lake,
deepening your spiritual wisdom.

Let the Spirit of Fire be with you
through the warmth of your heart.
May the Great Spirit empower you
with energy, joy and light.

May the Spirit of Earth be with you
keeping your body strong,
grounding your roots in firm foundations,
and a true sense of belonging, wherever you are.

May you be blessed.

Coming into Power

AFFIRMATION: I step into my power boldly and confidently.

You have been gathering your inner forces and are coming into your own strength. Assume your power. Accept the vibrant truth that all you need is already within you. It is safe to own your deepest inner gifts.

Editor's Acknowledgements

We offer our immense gratitude to each of the remarkable Soul Coaches who've shared their stories and wisdom throughout the pages of this book. Your gentle guidance and unique ways of listening for the whispers of the soul are truly inspirational. Many thanks too, to Fiona Raven for her assistance in crafting the design of this book.

Our heartfelt thanks go to Denise Linn for allowing us to use excerpts from her *Gateway Oracle Cards Guidebook*. We are deeply indebted to Denise who, in her infinite grace, created the soul-filled community which gave birth to these stories. Finally, we extend our deep gratitude and love to the authors' loved ones for their continued support on this journey, with special thanks to my son Marlon.

About Soul Wings® Press
Publishing for the Soul®

Soul Wings® Press is an award-winning Small Press Publisher.
We specialize in providing compassionate, professional editorial services
and quality book publishing to assist experts in the fields of
Self-help and Spirituality to become published authors.

If you wish to read interviews with our authors,
or become an author yourself, please visit our website:
www.SoulWingsPress.com

Soul Wings Press® Titles of related Interest

Soul Whispers: Collective Wisdom from Soul Coaches around the World ©2009
Soul Whispers II: Secret Alchemy of the Elements in Soul Coaching ©2011
Angels: Winged Whispers – True Stories from Angel Experts around the World ©2011
Planet Whispers: Wisdom from Soul Travelers around the World ©2011

Soul Wings® Press
Publishing for the Soul®
668 N Coast Hwy, Suite 234
Laguna Beach CA 92651 USA
125 Oxford Street, Suite 125
Bondi Junction NSW 2022 Australia
www.SoulWingsPress.com